Strawberries

CAPTURE THE ESSENCE

Strawberries

CAPTURE THE ESSENCE

by Carol Shirkey

NEW WIN PUBLISHING, INC.

Library of Congress Cataloging-in-Publication Data

Shirkey, Carol.
    Strawberries : capture the essence / by Carol Shirkey.
      p.   cm.
    Includes index.
    ISBN 0-8329-0466-X : $19.95
    1. Cookery (Strawberries)   I. Title.
TX813.S9S45 1992
641.6'475--dc20
                                                                    92-10770
                                                                    CIP

DEDICATION

I wish to thank all the persons who either directly or indirectly have assisted me in the preparation and compilation of this cookbook. Special recognition is extended to my husband, Robert, for his invaluable support and encouragement and to my sister-in-law, Mona, for her help and expertise.

TABLE OF CONTENTS

ACKNOWLEDGMENTS

The author wishes to thank the following people for their positive contributions to this book.

Line Art
Rhonda Houk
Robert Sokoloff
Sharon Firsick

Color Photography
Kevin Cozad

Table Settings
Michel Imber

Jacket Art
Robert Sokoloff

MOM'S EIGHT BEATITUDES

*Blessed is the salt added to sugar for cooked icing to
keep it from graining.*
Blessed is the soda that burns off cooking pans.
*Blessed is the vinegar that when added to sweet milk will
sour for immediately using.*
*Blessed is the butter rubbed along the top of the pan in which
chocolate or spaghetti is boiled; it will prevent boiling over.*
*Blessed is the pipe cleaner that cleans the little holes in
gas burners.*
*Blessed is the cornmeal that dry cleans light or white leather
gloves.*
*Blessed are the few drops of lemon juice added to dates, figs, or
raisins before running through the food chopper to prevent
clogging.*
*Blessed is the salt added to water when boiling eggs; it will keep
them from cracking.*

1. BEVERAGES, DIPS, SPREADS, SAUCES, FONDUES

The folks who deal in sunshine
Are the ones who get the crowds.
They do a lot more business
Than the fools who peddle clouds.

STRAWBERRY CREAM

For each serving, blend ½ pint vanilla ice cream and ½ cup chilled strawberry soda in blender or with rotary beater.

SNAPPY STRAWBERRY SODA

½ cup crushed strawberries
½ cup lemon juice
6 scoops vanilla ice cream
1 bottle (28 oz.) sparkling water, chilled

Combine strawberries and lemon juice. Divide evenly into six tall soda glasses. Add a scoop of ice cream to each glass and fill with chilled sparkling water, stirring to blend.

STRAWBERRY LEMONADE PUNCH

½ cup sugar
2 tsp. peppermint flavoring
2 cups boiling water
2 (10 oz.) packages frozen strawberries
5 cups water
2 (6 oz.) cans frozen pink lemonade concentrate, thawed and undiluted
½ gallon strawberry ice cream

Combine first 3 ingredients: stir to dissolve sugar and let stand 5 minutes. Add strawberries, stirring until thawed. Press strawberry mixture through a strainer; discard pulp. Add water and lemonade, stirring well. Chill thoroughly. Spoon ice cream into punch just before serving. Yields 4½ quarts.

STRAWBERRY ICE

4 cups fresh strawberries, hulled and cored
½ cup unsweetened orange juice
3 tbsp. honey

Combine all ingredients in an electric blender; process until smooth. Pour mixture into an 8-inch square pan. Cover and freeze until slushy. Spoon mixture into blender and process until smooth. Return to pan and freeze until firm. Serves 4.

STRAWBERRY SMOOTHIE

1 cup milk
½ pint vanilla ice cream
1 cup fresh strawberries
¼ cup honey

Whip all ingredients together by using a blender. If using electric mixer, berries should be mashed. Delicious served with pretzel sticks. Makes 2 shakes.

STRAWBERRY-YOGURT FROST

1 cup plain yogurt
¾ cup nonfat dry milk
¼ cup sugar
1 pkg. (16 oz.) frozen unsweetened strawberries

Place yogurt, dry milk, and sugar in blender. Blend on high speed 20 seconds. Add ½ cup strawberries. Blend on high speed 10 seconds, then stir. Repeat with remaining strawberries, using ½ cup at a time. Pour into glasses and serve with cocktail straws.

STRAWBERRY MILK SHAKE

1 pkg. (10 oz.) frozen strawberries
1 cup instant nonfat dry milk
4½ cups cold milk
1 qt. softened strawberry ice cream

Crush the thawed strawberries and add nonfat dry milk and whole milk. Blend thoroughly. Add softened ice cream and beat or shake just enough to blend ingredients. Pour into tall glasses and serve immediately. Makes 6 servings.

STRAWBERRY SHAKE
(72 calories per serving)

Looks and tastes like an ice cream shake!

2 cups unsweetened whole strawberries, fresh or frozen
1½ cups skim milk
2 tbsp. sugar
Dash ground cinnamon

If using fresh strawberries, halve larger berries and freeze in plastic bag. In blender container, combine milk, sugar, and cinnamon. Gradually add frozen berries. Blend on medium speed until smooth. Serve immediately. Serves 5.

STRAWBERRY OR RASPBERRY PUNCH

1 can (12½ oz.) frozen orange juice
1 can (12½ oz.) frozen lemonade
1 can (14 oz.) crushed pineapple and juice
4 cups home-frozen strawberries or raspberries, partially thawed,
*   or 4 pkgs. (10 oz.) commercially frozen strawberries or raspberries,*
*   partially thawed*
¼ cup lemon or lime concentrate
6 cups ginger ale
3 trays ice cubes

Shortly before serving, combine all ingredients. For a sweeter punch dissolve sugar in boiling water and add to punch. Makes 50 punch cups.

5

STRAWBERRY DAIQUIRIS

6 tbsp. light rum
¼ cup lime juice
2 tbsp. sugar
2 cups frozen whole strawberries, partially thawed

Combine in a blender the rum, lime juice, and sugar. Blend to dissolve sugar. Add partially thawed strawberries and blend until smooth. Serves 2.

BERRY-WHEAT GERM BEVERAGE

1 cup milk, cold
1 banana
1 tbsp. wheat germ
2 tbsp. strawberry or raspberry jam

Combine all ingredients in blender. Blend until smooth. Serves 2.

BERRY-YOGURT SHAKE

¾ cup fresh strawberries or raspberries
2 tbsp. honey
1 cup cold milk
1 cup yogurt

Puree berries in blender. Add remaining ingredients and blend until smooth. Note: Seed can be removed if desired by forcing puree through a sieve. Serves 2.

STRAWBERRY CHAMPAGNE-PUNCH FRUIT BOWL

4 cups fresh strawberries, hulled and cored
½ cup granulated sugar
1 bottle (4/5 quart) sauterne
1 cup cognac
Iced fruits for punch (see below)
4 bottles (4/5 quart) chilled champagne

Two hours before serving, sprinkle strawberries with sugar. Add sauterne and cognac. Refrigerate at least 2 hours. At serving time, arrange the iced fruits in a punch bowl, "trapping" nectarines, plums, and strawberries beneath one or two large bunches of grapes. Pour in berries with their liquid, then slowly add champagne. Serve a strawberry in each cup of punch. Makes 36½ cups.

ICED FRUITS FOR PUNCH

Frozen whole fruits will chill the punch as well as ice rings or ice cubes and are more colorful. Also, they will not dilute the punch. Strawberries, grapes, peaches, nectarines, plums, pears, apricots, lemons, and cherries can all be frozen successfully. Grapes and cherries stay close to the bottom, so use these on top of other fruits for anchorage. Freeze the fruits the night before they are to be used.

COLODA

2 cups crushed pineapple and juice
⅔ cup yogurt
¼ cup coconut liquer
1 cup fresh strawberries or 1 cup whole frozen strawberries, partly thawed

Place all ingredients in blender and blend until smooth. Add crushed ice and serve. Yields 3 cups.

TWO-BERRY SHRUB

2 cups home-frozen raspberries, thawed, or 2 pkgs (10 oz.) commercially
*   frozen raspberries, thawed*
2 cups home-frozen strawberries, thawed, or 2 pkgs. (10 oz.) commercially
*   frozen strawberries, thawed*
1 can (12½ oz.) frozen lemonade concentrate, just thawed
8 cups club soda, chilled

Combine raspberries and strawberries. Simmer 5 minutes. Strain and chill. Combine lemonade concentrate and club soda and add to fruit liquid. Serve over crushed ice. Serves 12.

FRUIT JUICE WITH STRAWBERRIES

3 qts. unsweetened pineapple juice
1 can (6 oz.) frozen orange juice
1 can (6 oz.) frozen lemon juice
½ cup sugar
3 large bottles ginger ale
1 pt. fresh or frozen strawberries
Lemon or lime slices

Combine fruit juices and sugar. Chill thoroughly. Add ginger ale and strawberries just before serving. Pour over cake of ice in punch bowl. Float thin slices of lemon or lime. Yields 65 servings.

STRAWBERRY SODAS

2 pts. fresh strawberries, hulled and cored
1 cup milk
¼ cup sugar
1 pt. vanilla ice cream, softened
1 qt. crushed ice
Club soda

Put strawberries in blender and puree. Then strain. Stir milk into the strawberry puree. Add the sugar and ice cream. Beat with electric mixer or use blender. Pour the mixture over some of the ice into soda glasses. Fill up with soda. Add remaining ice. Serve at once. Makes 6 sodas.

For an extra touch, serve sodas with a plate of glazed strawberries made by dipping whole dry berries into a mixture of heated cornstarch and water. Currant jelly heated and thinned with water may also be used. Use a wooden pick or skewer for dipping.

BRANDIED STRAWBERRIES WITH CREAM

2 pts. (2 pounds) strawberries, hulled and cored
1 cup heavy cream
3 tbsp. kirsch
1 cup sour cream
¼ cup dark or light brown sugar, firmly packed
3 oz. brandy or cognac

Whip the heavy cream until it just holds its shape. In a small bowl stir the kirsch into the sour cream and mix until smooth. Fold the two creams together. Cover and refrigerate.

Strawberries should be drained on paper towels and placed in a bowl. Add sugar and brandy and stir gently with a rubber spatula. Let stand for one hour, stirring occasionally. Cover and refrigerate.

To serve, place the berries in wine glasses or individual dessert bowls. Pour on any remaining marinade. Stir the cream gently and spoon generously over the berries.

CINNAMON CREAM CHEESE DIP OR SAUCE

1 cup cream cheese, softened
2 tbsp. brown sugar
1 tsp. cinnamon

Combine all ingredients. Yields 1 cup.

YOGURT-SOUR CREAM DIP

1 cup yogurt
1 cup sour cream
2 tbsp. honey
¾ tsp. ground ginger
½ tsp. lemon juice

Combine all ingredients. Cover and refrigerate one hour before serving. Yields 2 cups.

STRAWBERRY SPREAD

½ cup strawberry juice
1 pkg. (8 oz.) cream cheese, softened

Place juice and cream cheese in blender. Process until of spreading consistency. Spread on cooled strawberry bread. (See recipe at end of Part 2.)

LIGHT STRAWBERRY SPREAD

2 envelopes unflavored gelatin
1 cup unsweetened apple juice, divided in half
3 qts. fresh strawberries, washed, hulled, and cored
1 tbsp. lemon juice

Sprinkle gelatin over ½ cup apple juice and set aside. Combine remaining ½ cup apple juice, strawberries, and lemon juice in a Dutch oven. Cook over medium-low heat 10–15 minutes, stirring constantly. Mash strawberry mixture with a fork. Add the softened gelatin mixture, stirring until gelatin dissolves. Quickly spoon into hot sterilized jars, leaving ¼-inch headspace. Cover at once with metal lids and screw bands tight. Cool. Store in refrigerator for up to one month. Yields 6 one-half pints.

STRAWBERRY BUTTER

½ cup soft butter
⅓ cup powedered sugar
1 pkg. (10 oz.) frozen strawberries, thawed

Whip butter until creamy. Drain juice from thawed berries. Gradually add berries to butter, beating well after each addition. Beat in sugar. Chill until serving time. Yields 1½ cups.

CUSTARD SAUCE TO SERVE WITH STRAWBERRIES OR RASPBERRIES

4 egg yolks, beaten
⅓ cup sugar
⅛ tsp. salt
2 cups milk
1 tsp. vanilla

In double boiler combine egg yolks, sugar, and salt. Gradually add milk and cook and stir until custard coats the spoon. Remove from heat. Add vanilla. Yields 2¼ cups.

BERRY TOPPING

2 cups frozen, unsweetened strawberries or raspberries, thawed and drained
¼ cup juice from berries
3 egg yolks
2 tbsp. sugar
⅛ tsp. salt
¼ tsp. almond extract
2 cups whipped cream or prepared topping

In top of double boiler combine the juice from the berries, the egg yolks, sugar, and salt. Cook and stir until mixture is very thick. Add almond extract. Cover the surface with waxed paper and chill. Fold in whipped cream and berries. Yields 2¼ cups.

STRAWBERRY SAUCE

1 cup strawberries
½ cup sugar
1 tbsp. cornstarch
½ cup water
½ cup lemon juice
2 tbsp. butter

Puree strawberries in a blender and strain to remove seeds. Mix the sugar and cornstarch in a medium-sized saucepan. Gradually blend in the water. Stir over medium heat until the sauce thickens and boil for half a minute. Stir in lemon juice, butter, and strawberry puree. Chill.

STRAWBERRIES FLORIDA TOPPING

1 cup hulled, cored, and sliced strawberries
2 tbsp. orange juice
¼ tsp. grated orange rind

Mix strawberries with orange juice and grated orange rind. Serve over ice cream, or layer with scoops of ice cream in parfait glasses.

BANANA PANCAKES WITH STRAWBERRY SAUCE

1¾ cup flour
2½ tsp. baking powder
¼ tsp. salt
4 tbsp. brown sugar
1 egg, beaten
1¾ cup milk
1 tsp. vanilla
3 tbsp. butter or margarine, melted
2 bananas

Sift together flour, baking powder and salt. Add brown sugar. Mix together beaten egg, milk, vanilla and butter or margarine. Add liquid to dry ingredients. Cut bananas into thin slices and add to batter. Make pancakes as usual and serve with strawberry sauce (below).

Strawberry Sauce:
2 cups frozen unsweetened strawberries, thawed and drained
1 cup juice from strawberries (add water to make 1 cup)
3 tbsp. cornstarch
¾ cup sugar
2 tbsp. lemon juice

Combine the juice, cornstarch, and sugar. Cook until thick. Add lemon juice and strawberries. Serve warm on pancakes. Yields 16 pancakes.

BERRY AND CHERRY SAUCE

2 cups frozen, unsweetened strawberries or raspberries, thawed
1 tsp. lemon juice
1 can (19 oz.) cherry pie filling

Combine all ingredients and mix. With strawberries this sauce is mellow, and with raspberries it is more pungent.

KAHLUA SOUR CREAM SAUCE OR DIP

1 cup sour cream
2 tbsp. brown sugar
2 tbsp. Kahlua

Combine all ingredients. Yields 1 cup.

PEACHES WITH STRAWBERRY SAUCE

1½ cups frozen unsweetened strawberries, partially thawed and drained
1 tbsp. Grand Marnier or other orange-flavored liqueur
2 tbsp. unsweetened white grape juice or apple juice
2 cans (16 oz.) unsweetened sliced peaches, chilled and drained

Combine strawberries, liqueur, and grape juice in a blender. Blend until smooth. Spoon sauce into 4 individual serving dishes. Arrange 6 peach slices over the sauce in each dish. Reserve remaining peach slices for other uses. Yields 4 servings (about 74 calories per serving).

BRANDIED STRAWBERRY SAUCE

3 cups whole frozen strawberries, thawed and drained
½ cup juice from strawberries
1 tbsp. cornstarch
½ cup currant jelly
¼ cup brandy

Combine juice from strawberries with cornstarch. Melt jelly in a saucepan and gradually add cornstarch mixture. Cook and stir until thickened. Carefully fold in strawberries and brandy. Cover and refrigerate. Yields 2½ cups.

STRAWBERRY SYRUP

With blender or mixer, blend one package (10 oz.) frozen sliced strawberries, thawed, until smooth. In a saucepan combine the strawberries, ½ cup light corn syrup, and a dash of salt. Bring to a boil and boil gently while stirring constantly for 5 minutes. Serve warm. Makes 1½ cups syrup.

SPICED STRAWBERRY SAUCE

2 cups frozen strawberries, thawed and drained
1 cup juice from strawberries (add water to make 1 cup)
2 tbsp. cornstarch
¼ tsp. sugar
½ tsp. cloves
½ tsp. cinnamon
½ tsp. allspice

Combine juice from strawberries, cornstarch, and sugar. Cook and stir until mixture thickens. Add spices and fold in strawberries. Cover and refrigerate. Yields 2½ cups.

BERRIES IN CHEESE SAUCE

1 qt. strawberries, hulled and cored
2 pkgs. (3 oz.) cream cheese
4 tbsp. heavy cream
⅓ cup confectioner's sugar

Beat cream cheese until soft and smooth. Beat in cream and sugar and chill. About an hour before serving, select several unblemished strawberries for garnish and fold remainder into the cream-cheese sauce. Keep cold until ready to serve. Excellent with crusty French bread. Serves 4.

HOT STRAWBERRY SAUCE

1 pt. strawberries, hulled, cored, and halved,
*   or 1 pkg. frozen strawberries, thawed*
¼ cup sugar for fresh berries
1½ tbsp. Grand Marnier

In a saucepan, combine berries and sugar and simmer over low heat until just soft. Remove from heat and stir in the Grand Marnier. Serve immediately.

FRESH STRAWBERRIES IN HONEYED RASPBERRY SAUCE

Sauce:

1½ to 2 cups fresh raspberries
¼ cup honey

Wash raspberries very quickly and spread on paper towels to drain. Puree the berries and strain to remove seeds. Stir in the honey. Refrigerate sauce if you do not plan to use within a day or two.

For strawberries, use 4–6 cups. Wash, hull, and core them and drain on paper towels. Place in wine glasses or dessert bowls and spoon raspberry sauce over them. Serve cold or at room temperature.

FONDUE FOR STRAWBERRIES

A fondue consists of melted and blended ingredients. For dipping, have bite-size pieces of fresh pineapple, peaches, cake, and always the beautiful strawberries. Wash and drain strawberries but leave caps and stems on.

CHOCOLATE AND HONEY FONDUE

1 cup chocolate chips
½ cup cream or evaporated milk
¼ cup honey

Carefully heat all ingredients until blended.

MOCHA FONDUE

1 cup chocolate chips
1 tbsp. instant coffee
¾ cup cream or evaporated milk
1 tbsp. Tia Maria or Kahlua, optional

Carefully heat all ingredients until blended.

STRAWBERRY FONDUE

1 cup cream or evaporated milk
1 tbsp. cornstarch
¾ cup strawberries, pureed
½ cup confectioner's icing sugar

Combine cream or milk and cornstarch. Add pureed strawberries and confectioner's icing sugar. Heat and blend until mixture thickens. Serve with bite-size pieces of fruit, French bread, cake, or biscuits. Yields 2 cups.

FONDANT-DIPPED STRAWBERRIES

2½ cups confectioner's icing sugar
3 tbsp. lemon juice
2 tbsp. light corn syrup
30 strawberries, washed and drained, caps and stems on

In top of double boiler, combine confectioner's icing sugar, lemon juice and corn syrup. Cook and stir until mixture is smooth and of a consistency that will coat a strawberry. Remove from heat but keep warm over hot water. Hold strawberry by stem and dip into mixture, turning to cover the entire berry. Dry the berries on wire racks placed on cookie sheets. Strawberries should dry for one hour but should not be stored overnight. Yields 30.

CHOCOLATE-DIPPED STRAWBERRIES I

Note: Dipped strawberries should be refrigerated just long enough to set the chocolate. Do not store in the refrigerator.

3 oz. semisweet chocolate
1 tbsp. unsalted butter
1 tsp. cognac or brandy
12 large strawberries

In a double boiler, combine the chocolate, butter, and cognac over moderate heat. Melt the mixture, stirring frequently until smooth, about 5 minutes. Remove from heat. Cover a small platter or large flat plate with a sheet of waxed paper. Holding onto the hull, dip a strawberry half way into the chocolate and place on the prepared platter. Repeat with the remaining berries and chocolate. Refrigerate until set, about 10 minutes. Store in a cool place for up to 24 hours.

CHOCOLATE-DIPPED STRAWBERRIES II

8 large strawberries with leaves intact
1 pkgs. (6 oz.) semisweet chocolate chips, melted
½ cup chilled whipping cream
1 tbsp. cherry brandy

Cover each strawberry one fourth of the way with melted chocolate (leaves and top of strawberry should be visible). Place on waxed paper. Refrigerate uncovered until chocolate is firm, about 30 minutes. Beat whipping cream and brandy in chilled 1½ quart bowl until stiff. Divide whipped cream among four dishes. Top each with 2 chocolate-dipped strawberries. Serves 4.

For white chocolate-dipped strawberries with this recipe, use two 2-ounce squares ᶠ white chocolate candy coating, melted, in place of the chocolate chips.

DOUBLE-DIPPED STRAWBERRIES

Dip berries no more than 2 hours before serving.

Vanilla-flavored candy coating (at least 2 oz.)
Fresh strawberries, rinsed and patted dry
Semisweet chocolate or chocolate-flavored candy coating (2 oz. min.)

In small saucepan melt the vanilla candy coating over low heat, stirring constantly. Remove from heat. Holding berry by its green cap, dip a portion of the fruit into the melted vanilla coating. Let excess coating drop off berry. Place on a baking sheet lined with waxed paper and let dry.

In another small saucepan, melt chocolate over low heat, stirring constantly. Dip strawberry in melted chocolate, leaving part of the white coating showing. Let dry and then chill.

STRAWBERRIES DIPPED IN WHITE CHOCOLATE

¾ pound white chocolate, cut into pieces
30 large strawberries

Put chocolate in saucepan and melt slowly while stirring over direct heat (or over simmering water). Remove from burner when melted. Hold berries by stem end and dip pointed ends into white chocolate halfway up the berry. Twist the berry to remove excess chocolate. Place on a baking sheet lined with waxed paper. Refrigerate 10–15 minutes to set.

2. CREPES, CUSTARDS, BARS, MUFFINS, BREAD

I'm sorry for people,
wherever they are, who
live in a home where
there's no cookie jar.

STRAWBERRY CREPES

2 cups fresh strawberries, hulled, cored, and sliced
1 cup buttermilk baking mix
1 egg
1 cup milk
½ cup granulated sugar (only if using fresh strawberries)
1 cup dairy sour cream
½ cup brown sugar (packed)

Beat baking mix, egg, and milk with rotary beater until smooth. Lightly grease a 6 or 7-inch skillet. Heat the skillet until a few drops water sprinkled on it "skitter" around. Pour 2 tablespoons batter into hot skillet, rotating the pan until batter covers the bottom. Cook until light brown, then turn and brown the other side. Place crepes between paper towels until ready to fill.

Filling:

Sprinkle sliced strawberries with the sugar and refrigerate. Mix sour cream and brown sugar. Place one tablespoon sour cream mixture on each crepe. Roll up and place seam side down on oven-proof serving platter. Cover with aluminum foil. When main course is served, turn off oven. Heat crepes during the meal. Serve warm with sweetened strawberries. May substitute two packages (10 oz.) frozen sliced strawberries and omit the sugar. Note: To flame, heat the sweetened strawberries in a chafing dish just until warm. Warm 2 tablespoons orange-flavored liqueur or brandy. Pour it over the strawberries and ignite.

23

STRAWBERRY CREAM CREPES

1 pt. fresh strawberries, halved and sweetened to taste
2 eggs
⅔ cup milk
1 tbsp. melted shortening
½ cup sifted flour
¼ tsp. salt
1 tsp. sugar
Oil or shortening for griddle

Beat eggs thoroughly, then add milk and shortening. Sift flour with salt and sugar. Add it to egg mixture and beat until smooth. Heat a little oil or shortening on a pan or griddle. Drop the crepe batter in the pan in 5-inch rounds. Cook, turning once, until light brown on both sides. To serve: Spoon sweetened halved strawberries, then a level tablespoonful of whipped cream down the side of each crepe. Roll up and place seam side down on a serving platter. Sprinkle with confectioner's sugar.

STRAWBERRY COTTAGE CHEESE FILLING FOR CREPES

3 cups strawberries, fresh,
*   or 3 cups whole frozen strawberries, thawed and drained*
1 cup low-fat cottage cheese
1 tbsp. sugar
½ tsp. vanilla

Combine in mixer or blender one cup strawberries, cottage cheese, sugar, and vanilla. Mix until smooth. If fresh strawberries are used, the remaining 2 cups should be sliced. Place strawberries in crepes and serve with the sauce. Serves 8.

HUNGARIAN BERRY PANCAKES

2 cups sour cream
1 egg, beaten
½ tsp. ground ginger
2 cups sifted all-purpose flour
2 cups sliced strawberries, sweetened to taste
¾ cup blanched, shredded, and toasted almonds
¼ tsp. salt

24

Combine sour cream, egg, salt, and ginger. Stir in flour and beat until batter is blended. It should be the consistency of thick cream. Adjust consistency by adding a little milk or more flour. Heat a small frying pan, brush it with butter and pour in a spoonful of batter. Tip the pan so batter will flow evenly over the bottom and cook for one minute. Turn and brown the other side lightly. Slide the baked pancakes onto a floured board and continue to bake cakes until all batter is used. When ready to serve, put a spoonful of strawberries in the center of each pancake and roll up. Place in a buttered oven-proof shallow pan. Sprinkle with almonds and glaze in a hot oven or under the broiler until pancakes blister, but be careful they do not burn. Makes 24.

STRAWBERRY FRITTERS

These petite fritters are a very special treat served at breakfast or brunch.

1 jar (12 oz.) apricot preserves
2 pts. fresh strawberries (whole and completely dry)
2 cups ground walnuts or pecans
2 eggs slightly beaten
2 cups finely crushed saltines
Fat for deep frying heated to 365 degrees

Force the preserves through a sieve. Gently but firmly grasp each berry by the hull and dip in preserves. Using a fork to help coat, cover berry up to the hull with preserves and allow the excess to drop through the tines of the fork. Coat with nuts, still holding the hull, and shake gently. Dip in beaten eggs, smoothing off the excess, and then coat with cracker crumbs up to the hull. Place on a wire rack and chill 30 minutes to set coating. Fry berries, 6–8 at a time, in the hot fat until golden brown (less than one minute). Be sure that temperature of fat is heated to 365 degrees after each frying. Carefully remove berries with slotted spoon and drain on paper towel-lined rack. Serve warm with powdered sugar.

JAM CUSHIONS

1 pkg. (8 oz.) cream cheese
1 cup butter or margarine
2 cups flour, sifted
1 cup finely chopped nuts
1 cup strawberry or raspberry jam

Preheat oven to 400 degrees. Blend cream cheese and butter and stir in flour to make a dough. Chill 3 hours. Prepare filling by combining the nuts and jam. When dough has chilled, divide into 4 pieces and work with one piece at a time. Roll out thin and cut into 2-inch circles. Top the center of the circle with a scant teaspoon of nut and jam mixture. Cover with another circle and seal edges by pressing with a fork. Bake 12–15 minutes. Yields 48.

CHEESE SQUARES

½ cup butter or margarine
½ cup grated Velveeta cheese
¼ cup brown sugar
1¾ cups flour
1½ tsp. baking powder
½ tsp. salt
½ cup strawberry or raspberry jam

Preheat oven to 300 degrees. Combine all the ingredients except the jam to form a crumb mixture. Pat ¾ of mixture into 8 × 8-inch pan. Spread with the jam. Sprinkle the rest of the crumb mixture over the top. Bake about 25 minutes. Yields 25 pieces.

STRAWBERRY COBBLER

4 cups frozen strawberries, thawed and drained
1 cup juice from strawberries (with water if needed)
¾ cup sugar
2 tbsp. cornstarch
2 tbsp. lemon juice
½ tsp. cinnamon
2 cups flour
2 tbsp. sugar
1 tsp. salt
6 tbsp. shortening
½ cup milk

Preheat oven to 375 degrees. Combine juice, sugar, and cornstarch and cook in sauce pan until mixture thickens. Add lemon juice, cinnamon, and strawberries. Pour into greased 1½-quart casserole or baking pan. Combine remaining ingredients to make biscuit dough and drop by spoonfuls into fruit. Bake 35–40 minutes. Serves 6.

ELEGANT CUSTARD

4 cups strawberries
¼ cup anise-flavored liqueur or favorite liqueur
¾ cup flour
4 eggs
1 cup sugar
4 cups milk, boiling
1 cup whipping cream

Combine strawberries and liqueur and chill several hours. The strawberries may be slightly sweetened if desired. In a saucepan combine flour, eggs, and sugar. Slowly add the boiling milk, using a wire whisk to combine. Cook and stir until mixture thickens. Cool. Whip the cream and use the whisk to combine with custard. Layer strawberries and custard in your fine stemware. (Raspberries can be used in place of strawberries.) Serves 8.

STRAWBERRY-RHUBARB CRUNCH

Base:

¾ cup sugar
1½ tbsp. mint tapioca
1½ cups whole frozen strawberries, thawed or drained
½ cup juice from strawberries (with water if needed)
3 cups diced rhubarb

Topping:

¼ cup butter or margarine, melted
1 cup quick-cooking rolled oats
½ cup flour
¾ cup brown sugar
1 tsp. cinnamon
½ cup chopped nuts

Preheat oven to 375 degrees. Combine base ingredients in 2-quart baking dish. Let stand 5 minutes. Combine topping ingredients and sprinkle over base. Bake about 25 minutes or until rhubarb is cooked.

EGGS A LA NEIGE

4 cups milk
6 egg whites
1¼ cups granulated sugar
Salt
1½ cups heavy cream
¾ tsp. vanilla extract
6 egg yolks
1½ tbsp. flour
2 pints fresh strawberries
1 sq. unsweetened chocolate

Scald the milk in a large skillet early in the day or the previous day. Beat the egg whites until frothy and gradually add ¾ cup sugar and ¼ teaspooon salt, beating until stiff. Heat the milk and drop in 3 large mounds of meringue (the egg white mixture), 1-inch apart. Cook 5 minutes, turning once with slotted spoon. Drain on paper towel. Repeat this process until all meringue is used. Meringues must be kept refrigerated until 20 minutes before serving.

Scald in a double boiler the cream with vanilla and 1½ cups of the milk used in cooking the meringues. Meanwhile, beat the yolks until light, and then beat in ½ cup sugar, a pinch of salt, the flour, and a little of the hot cream-milk mixture. Stir this mixture into the rest of the hot cream-milk mixture. Cook over hot (not boiling) water while stirring until the custard sauce coats a metal spoon. Custard should be kept refrigerated (along with meringues) until 20 minutes before serving.

Hull and core the strawberries and slice them into a deep serving dish. Heap the chilled meringues over the strawberries and pour on custard. Shave the unsweetened chocolate over all. Serves 8.

STRAWBERRIES AND CUSTARD

1 cup grated blanched almonds
1½ cups sweet white wine
4 egg yolks
½ cup granulated sugar
Confectioners' sugar
Whipped cream, tinted a delicate pink
Red currant jelly
Strawberries, hulled and cored

Heat almonds and white wine over simmering water. In a saucepan beat egg yolks and granulated sugar until sugar is dissolved. Gradually whisk in wine and almonds. Pour into a buttered and sugared 8-inch layer cake pan, set in a larger pan containing about 1-inch hot water. Bake in preheated 325-degree oven for about 45 minutes, or until silver knife blade comes out clean. Cool and chill.

To serve: Unmold custard on a chilled platter and arrange a pyramid of strawberries, rolled in confectioners' sugar, in the center. Surround strawberries with a crown of pink whipped-cream rosettes. Keep cold until serving time and before serving surround with a ribbon of red currant jelly which has been heated and thinned to sauce consistency with sweet white wine or water. Serves 4.

CREAM-FILLED STRAWBERRIES
(To be used as a garnish, or served 4–5 in a fruit dish.)

24 large strawberries
1 cup whipping cream
2 tbsp. almond or orange liqueur
¼ cup confectioner's icing sugar

Wash and drain strawberries. Leave caps on. Slit each berry into quarters, working toward the cap but not cutting through it. Whip the cream and add flavoring. Use a pastry bag with a star tip to fill the strawberries. Dust with icing sugar. Serve within 3 hours. Yields 24.

DREAM BARS

Crust:
1 cup flour
¾ tsp. baking soda
¼ tsp. salt
1 cup rolled oats
½ cup brown sugar
½ cup butter or margarine

Filling:
1 cup strawberry or raspberry jam

Topping:
2 eggs, beaten
1 cup brown sugar
½ cup coconut
½ cup chopped nuts

Preheat oven to 350 degrees. Combine the first 6 ingredients to make a crumb mixture. Pat into a greased 9 × 13-inch pan. Spread jam on top. Combine eggs, brown sugar, and coconut and carefully pour over the jam. Sprinkle nuts on top. Bake about 30 minutes. Yields 54 squares.

JAM BARS

Crust:
1 cup flour, sifted
1 tsp. baking powder
½ cup butter or margarine
1 egg

Topping:
¾ cup sugar
1 tbsp. butter
1 egg
2 cups coconut

Filling:
1 cup strawberry or raspberry jam

Preheat oven to 325 degrees. Combine all crust ingredients and pat into bottom of greased 9 × 13-inch pan. Spread with the jam. Mix topping ingredients together and carefully spoon over the jam. Bake about 30 minutes, until brown. Yields 54 bars.

WALNUT MERINGUE BARS

1 cup butter or margarine
½ cup sugar
1 egg yolk
½ tsp. salt
2½ cups flour, sifted
1 cup strawberry or raspberry jam
4 egg whites
1 cup sugar
1 tsp. almond extract
¾ cup finely ground nuts

Preheat oven to 350 degrees. Cream butter and ½ cup sugar. Add egg yolk, salt, and flour and combine. Put into a 10 × 15-inch jelly roll pan and spread the jam over this base. Beat the egg whites until foamy and gradually add, while beating, the cup of sugar. Beat until stiff peaks form. Add almond extract and ground nuts. Spread the meringue (the egg whites and sugar) over the jelly layer, sealing to edges of dough. Bake 35–40 minutes until browned. Cut into squares while warm. Yields 36 squares.

HARVEST MUFFINS

2½ cups flour
½ cup sugar
2 tbsp. lard
2 tbsp. butter or margarine
2½ tsp. cream of tartar
1¼ tsp. baking soda
½ tsp. salt
1 cup milk
Butter or margarine for spreading sugar

Preheat oven to 375 degrees. Combine first 8 ingredients to make a soft dough. Roll out dough to ½" thickness. Spread with butter and sprinkle with sugar. Roll as for jelly roll and cut into equal pieces. Place in 9 × 13-inch pan. Place one teaspoon jam filling on each piece (recipe below). Bake 25–30 minutes.

Filling

¼ cup butter or margarine, melted
¼ cup sugar
½ to ¾ cup strawberry or raspberry jam

Makes 8–10 muffins.

STRAWBERRY BREAD

3 cups flour
1 tsp. baking soda
1 tsp. cinnamon
2 cups sugar
1 tsp. salt
2 pkgs. (10 oz. each) frozen strawberries, sliced
1¼ cups vegetable oil
4 eggs, well beaten
1 cup chopped pecans

Reserve ½ cup strawberry juice for spread. Mix all dry ingredients together. Make a hole in the center of mixture. Pour strawberries, oil, and eggs into the hole. Mix by hand until all ingredients are thoroughly combined. Stir in the chopped pecans. Pour into two greased and floured 9 × 5 × 3-inch pans. Bake at 350 degrees for 40–60 minutes.

Note: Spread slices of cooled bread with strawberry spread. (See recipes in Part 1.)

3. SOUPS, SANDWICHES, SALADS, PIZZA

When you have set the table with
Those things that taste so good,
We always are devourin' more
Than anybody should.
You say it makes you happy
Just because we like to eat,
But how can anyone resist
Such culinary treats?

STRAWBERRY SOUP I

4 pkgs. (10 oz.) commercially frozen strawberries, thawed
*   or 3 cups home-frozen, unsweetened strawberries, thawed and drained, plus*
*   2 cups juice from berries and ¼ cup sugar*
2 cups sweet wine
2 cinnamon sticks (2 inches ea.)
2 tsp. cornstarch
½ cup water

Combine commercially frozen strawberries (or home-frozen plus juice and sugar) with wine and cinnamon sticks. Simmer about 10 minutes. Combine cornstarch and water and slowly add to berry liquid. Simmer until mixture thickens. Remove cinnamon and refrigerate in covered container. Serves 6.

STRAWBERRY SOUP II

4 cups (3 pints) fresh strawberries, washed, hulled, and cored
½ cup sugar or 4 tbsp. honey
2 tsp. arrowroot
1 cup orange juice
1 cup Bordeaux wine
1 cup sour cream
6 strawberries for garnish

Place berries and sugar or honey in blender, and puree. Dissolve arrowroot in 2 tablespoons of orange juice and add to strawberry puree with remaining orange juice. Place mixture in a saucepan and cook over low heat, stirring constantly until the arrowroot has cooked and soup thickens. Remove from heat and add wine. Refrigerate. Serve the soup chilled, topped with sour cream and garnished with a strawberry.

STRAWBERRY SOUP III

4 cups fresh strawberries
    or 4 cups frozen whole strawberries, partly thawed
1 cup orange juice
2 tsp. instant tapioca
⅛ tsp. allspice
⅛ tsp. cinnamon
½ cup sugar
1 tsp. grated lemon peel
1 tbsp. lemon juice
1 cup buttermilk

Puree strawberries. Combine puree with orange juice in a saucepan. Remove about ¼ cup of mixture and combine with the tapioca. Add tapioca mixture to puree in saucepan. Add allspice, cinnamon, and sugar, and cook and stir until mixture thickens. Remove from heat. Add lemon peel, lemon juice, and buttermilk. Cover and refrigerate 8 hours or overnight. Serves 4.

STRAWBERRY SOUP IV — BLENDER QUICK

½ cup white wine
½ cup sugar
2 tbsp. lemon juice
1 tsp. grated lemon peel
2 cups strawberries, fresh,
    or 2 cups whole frozen strawberries, partly thawed

Combine all ingredients in a blender and blend until smooth. Cover and refrigerate. When soup is made with partly thawed berries, it is ready to serve without additional chilling. Serves 3.

FRUIT SOUP

3 tbsp. sugar
3 tbsp. cornstarch
⅛ tsp. salt
1¼ cups sparkling red wine
1 cup water
1½ cups cranberry juice
3 cups fresh strawberries or raspberries

Combine sugar, cornstarch, salt, wine, and water in a saucepan. Cook and stir. Simmer about one minute, then remove from heat and add cranberry juice. Cover and refrigerate. Strawberries or raspberries should be added when the soup is served. Use the soup the day it is prepared. Serves 6.

COLD CRANBERRY SOUP

2 oranges
1 tbsp. butter
1¼ cups sugar
1 cup sherry
1 pound fresh or frozen cranberries
1 cup dry Sauterne
1 cup half-and-half
1 cup sour cream
1 cup club soda, thoroughly chilled
16 pecan halves (garnish)

Carefully pare peel from oranges and cut into slivers. Juice the oranges, discarding membrane and pulp. Melt butter in a 3-quart saucepan over low heat. Sauté orange peel gently 2 minutes. Add sugar, sherry, and orange juice and let boil 2 minutes. Add cranberries. Cover and boil 2 minutes; uncover and boil 3 more minutes. Let cool, then cover and refrigerate at least 2 hours or, preferably, overnight.

Add Sauterne to chilled soup. Transfer to blender (in 1 batch if necessary) and mix at medium speed 1 minute. Add half-and-half and sour cream and blend 1 minute longer. Strain into large bowl and chill thoroughly. Before serving, add soda and mix well. Serve in cups over crushed ice, garnishing each serving with 2 pecan halves.

STRAWBERRY SANDWICH

½ cup cottage cheese
¼ cup sour cream
2 oz. cream cheese
8 slices bread of choice
1½ cups sliced strawberries

Combine and mix well the cottage cheese, sour cream, and cream cheese. Spread about 2 tablespoons of the mixture on bread. Cut the bread as desired. Top with overlapping slices of strawberries. Serves 8.

BERRY BLINTZ SANDWICHES

1½ cups creamed cottage cheese
1 egg
2 tbsp. sugar
12 slices bread, white or whole wheat
3 eggs
⅓ cup milk
2 cups home-frozen strawberries or raspberries, thawed,
*   or 2 pkgs. (10 oz.) commercially frozen strawberries or raspberries, thawed*
*   (sugar optional)*

Combine cottage cheese, one egg, and sugar until well mixed. Spread 6 slices of bread with the mixture and cover with remaining slices. In a shallow dish, combine 3 eggs with milk and mix. Preheat a large skillet with butter. Dip sandwiches into egg mixture on one side and then the other. Cook in skillet, browning both sides. Keep warm in oven until all are browned. Serve with strawberries or raspberries. Adjust sugar to taste. Serves 6.

40

SANDWICH LOAF

1 loaf unsliced brown bread
10 oz. whipped cream cheese
1 cup crushed pineapple, drained
¼ cup sunflower seeds
6 oz. gouda cheese, thinly sliced
3 kiwi fruit, sliced
1 cup strawberries, sliced

Remove crusts from bread. Slice horizontally into 3 layers. Spread each layer with whipped cream cheese. On the bottom layer, spread crushed pineapple and sprinkle with sunflower seeds; on second layer, the sliced cheese; on top layer, sliced kiwi fruit and strawberries. Stack the slices together. Refrigerate. Cut into 2-inch pieces at serving time. Serves 5. Note: Bread crusts can be frozen for later use as a dressing or bread pudding.

STRAWBERRY SALAD

½ lb. marshmallows
2 tbsp. milk
1 cup crushed strawberries, fresh or frozen
1 cup crushed pineapple (well drained)
1 pkg. (3 oz.) cream cheese
½ cup mayonnaise
1 cup whipping cream, whipped

Melt marshmallows in milk on top of double boiler. Cool, but not too long; add fruits. Mash cream cheese with a fork, blending until creamy. Blend mayonnaise and whipped cream with cream cheese. Fold into fruit and marshmallow mixture. Pour into a refrigerator tray and freeze until firm. Serve in slices or squares on crisp lettuce. Serves 8–10. Garnish with mayonnaise if desired.

STRAWBERRY GELATIN SALAD I

1 pkg. (3 oz.) strawberry gelatin
1 carton (8 oz.) whipped topping
1 small carton cottage cheese
1 can pineapple, drained
2 bananas, sliced

Mix all together in a large bowl and refrigerate until chilled. Then enjoy.

STRAWBERRY GELATIN SALAD II

2 pkgs. strawberry gelatin
1 cup water
2 pkgs. (10 oz. each) frozen strawberries
1 can (20 oz.) crushed pineapple
3 medium bananas, mashed
1 cup nuts (or amount desired)
1 pint sour cream

Prepare gelatin in cup of hot water. Add all other ingredients except nuts and sour cream and mix well. Pour half of mixture into a 12 × 8-inch pan and refrigerate until firm. Then spoon sour cream onto the gelatin mixture, adding chopped nuts. Pour rest of gelatin on top and chill. Serves 12.

STRAWBERRY DREAM WHIP SALAD

1 pkg. (6 oz.) strawberry gelatin
1 pkg. (12 oz.) frozen strawberries
1 pkg. Dream Whip

Prepare gelatin as directed, leaving out 1 cup of water and substituting the berries instead. Set until slightly firm, then add strawberries and let set until completely firm. Prepare Dream Whip as directed and mix with an electric mixer. Serve as either a salad or dessert.

STRAWBERRY CHIFFON SALAD

1 pkg. (3 oz.) strawberry gelatin
¾ cup boiling water
1 cup ice cubes
1 cup sliced fresh strawberries

1 pkg. (3 oz.) strawberry gelatin
¾ cup boiling water
1 cup ice cubes
2 cups whipped topping, thawed, or 2 cups prepared Dream Whip topping

Dissolve one package gelatin in ¾ cup boiling water. Add one cup ice cubes and stir about 3 minutes, until gelatin is slightly thickened. Remove any unmelted ice. Stir in fruit. Pour into a 5-cup mold. Place in refrigerator. Dissolve second package of gelatin in ¾ cup boiling water. Add ice cubes and stir about 3 minutes until gelatin is slightly thickened. Remove any unmelted ice. Fold in whipped topping. Pour into mold over fruited layer. Refrigerate at least one hour. Makes about 5 cups or 10 servings.

ROSY STRAWBERRY RING

2 pkgs. (3 oz.) strawberry-flavored gelatin
2 cups boiling water
2 pkgs (10 oz.) frozen sliced strawberries
1 can (13 oz.) crushed pineapple
2 large ripe bananas, peeled and finely diced
2 tbsp. lemon juice

Dissolve gelatin in boiling water. Add berries, stirring occasionally until thawed. Stir in pineapple, bananas, and lemon juice. Pour into a 6½-cup mold. Chill until firm, about 5–6 hours. Serve with sour cream dressing. Serves 8.

Sour cream dressing:

1 cup sour cream
1 tsp. sugar
¼ tsp. ground ginger
Dash salt

Combine dressing ingredients, mixing thoroughly, and chill.

STRAWBERRY MOLD

1 large pkg. strawberry gelatin
1 cup boiling water
1 quart strawberries
1 small pkg. cream cheese
Chopped nuts as desired

Prepare gelatin and pour over frozen strawberries. Cut the cream cheese into squares, roll in chopped nuts, and drop in a gelatin mold. Pour the strawberry/gelatin mixture into the mold and chill until firm.

STRAWBERRY LAYER GELATIN SALAD

First Layer:
1 pkg. (3 oz.) strawberry gelatin
1 cup boiling water
1 box (10 oz.) frozen strawberries

Prepare gelatin and add the strawberries. Pour into a pan and let set until firm.

Second Layer:
1 box (3 oz.) lemon gelatin
1 cup boiling water

Mix and set aside to thicken. Meanwhile, cream a 3-ounce package of cream cheese with ½ cup pineapple juice. Fold in 1 can crushed pineapple, drained. Whip one cup cream and fold in. Add to thickened lemon gelatin and pour over the strawberry layer. Chill completely before serving.

FROSTED STRAWBERRY SALAD

2 pkg. (3 oz. each) strawberry gelatin
2 cups boiling water
1 pkg. (10 oz.) frozen strawberries
1 small can crushed pineapple
3 bananas, mashed
1 pkg. (3 oz.) cream cheese
3 tbsp. mayonnaise

Dissolve gelatin in water. Add the frozen strawberries. Mix in pineapple and mashed bananas. Pour into an 8 × 12-inch pan. Let set until firm. Whip cream cheese with mayonnaise and frost top.

STRAWBERRY RHUBARB MOLD

Combine:
1 lb. frozen strawberries, defrosted and drained
1 lb. frozen rhubarb, cooked
20-oz. can crushed pineapple, drained

Dissolve:
2 pkgs. (3 oz.) strawberry gelatin in
1 cup boiling water

Combine juices from 3 fruits to make 3 cups liquid, adding water if necessary. Add to gelatin. Chill until slightly thickened. Add fruits and pour into 2-quart ring mold. Chill until firm; unmold to serve. Note: Always use canned pineapple with gelatin. Fresh pineapple will not jell.

LIME-STRAWBERRY SURPRISE SALAD

1 pkg. (10 oz.) frozen strawberries
1 pkg. (3 oz.) strawberry gelatin
1 pkg. (3 oz.) lime gelatin
1 cup crushed pineapple, drained
¼ cup mayonnaise
1 pkg. (8 oz.) cream cheese, softened
1 pkg. dessert topping mix
½ cup chopped nuts (or as desired)

Prepare lime gelatin as directed on the package. Chill until slightly thickened, then fold in the drained pineapple. Pour into an 8-inch square pan and chill until firm. Gradually add the mayonnaise to the softened cream cheese, mixing well. Prepare dessert topping mix according to directions and fold in the cream cheese and nuts. Spread over molded gelatin layer. Chill until firm.

Prepare strawberry gelatin as directed on the package. Chill until slightly thickened, then fold in the thawed strawberries. Chill until partially set and then pour over the cream cheese layer. Chill until firm.

CHRISTMAS JELLIED SALAD

First layer:

2 cups frozen strawberries, thawed and drained
1½ cups juice from strawberries (including water if needed)
1 pkg. (3 oz.) strawberry gelatin

Dissolve the strawberry gelatin in one cup of hot juice. Add remaining juice and chill until thick but not set. Add the strawberries. Pour into a 1½-quart clear dish. Refrigerate until almost set.

Second layer:

1 can (14 oz.) crushed pineapple, well drained
1¾ cups pineapple juice (including water if needed)
1 pkg. (3 oz.) lime gelatin
½ cup shredded cheddar cheese

Dissolve lime gelatin in one cup of hot juice. Add remaining juice and chill until thick but not set. Add pineapple and shredded cheese. Carefully pour over the first layer. Refrigerate until firm.

Third layer:

1 cup whipped cream or whipped topping
½ cup chopped nuts

Spread the whipped cream on top and sprinkle with chopped nuts. Serves 8.

STRAWBERRY-SOUR CREAM SALAD I

1 pkg. (3 oz.) strawberry gelatin
1 cup boiling water
1 pkg. (10 oz.) frozen strawberries
1 cup sour cream
1 cup chopped pecans

Dissolve the gelatin in boiling water. Add frozen strawberries. Stir until strawberries separate and thaw. Pour half of this mixture into a mold and chill until set. Mix the sour cream and pecans and spread over the strawberry layer. Add remaining strawberry mixture and chill until firm. Yields 6–8 servings.

STRAWBERRY-SOUR CREAM SALAD II

2 pkgs. (3 oz.) strawberry gelatin
2 cups boiling water (pineapple juice plus water to make 2 cups)
1 small can crushed pineapple, drained
2 bananas, mashed
1 pkg. (10 oz.) frozen strawberries
1 cup sour cream

Dissolve gelatin and add the remaining ingredients except sour cream. Pour half the mixture into a square pan and let set until firm. Spread sour cream over the gelatin fruit mixture. Over this, spoon or pour the rest of the partially congealed fruit mixture. Chill until firm.

STRAWBERRY OR RASPBERRY TUNA TOSSED SALAD

1 medium head of lettuce
1 can (6.5 oz.) tuna, drained
2 cups strawberries, halved, or raspberries
¼ cup slivered almonds
1 tbsp. chopped parsley

Dressing:
2 tbsp. orange juice
1 tbsp. grated orange peel
½ cup mayonnaise
⅛ tsp. salt
⅛ tsp. pepper

Break lettuce into bite-sized pieces. Put into a salad bowl. Sprinkle the tuna, strawberries (or raspberries), nuts, and parsley over lettuce. Blend together the salad dressing ingredients. Add to the salad and toss gently. Serves 4.

STRAWBERRY CHICKEN SALAD IN PITA BREAD

2 cups diced, cooked chicken
1 cup shredded lettuce
¾ cup white grapes, halved
1 cup strawberries, halved
1 cup sprouts
4 pita bread pockets

Combine salad ingredients. Add choice of dressing and stuff into pita bread pockets. Serves 4.

STRAWBERRY SHRIMP SALAD

2 lbs. cooked large shrimp, shelled and deveined
2 papayas or melons, sliced
½ pineapple, cut into spears
2 avocados, sliced
2 kiwi fruit, sliced
2 cups strawberries
Toasted coconut, slivered almonds, or macadamia nuts
Mint, optional

Arrange shrimp and fruit on salad greens. Garnish with mint, if using. Serve salad dressing in an attractive dish. Have small dishes of toasted coconut and slivered almonds or macadamia nuts to pass with salad dressing.

Salad dressing:
1 tbsp. crystallized ginger
½ cup whipping cream
2 tbsp. lime juice
1 tbsp. grated lime rind
2 tbsp. honey
¼ cup mayonnaise

Grate the ginger in a blender. Add whipping cream, lime juice, rind, and honey and blend until fluffy. Fold mixture into the mayonnaise. Serves 6.

STRAWBERRY SPINACH SALAD

1 bunch fresh spinach, washed and dried
1 cup quartered fresh strawberries

In a large salad bowl, place fresh spinach and tear into bite-size pieces. Add strawberries. Toss lightly with commercial creamy coleslaw dressing, mayonnaise, or your choice of dressing. Add a dash of salt and freshly ground pepper. Serves 4.

STRAWBERRY ZUCCHINI SALAD

A different way to serve some of that plentiful zucchini!

Leaf lettuce
1 cup thinly sliced zucchini
1½ cups halved strawberries

Place several pieces of leaf lettuce on a salad plate. Add thin slices of zucchini and halved strawberries. Serve with your favorite dressing. Serves 4.

PRETZEL SALAD

2⅔ cups pretzels, broken in small pieces
1½ cups butter or margarine, melted
4 pkgs. (3 oz.) cream cheese, softened
1¼ cups sugar
1 carton (9 oz.) frozen whipped topping, thawed
1 pkg. (6 oz.) strawberry gelatin
2 cups pineapple juice or water
2-3 cups fresh strawberries
*   or 1 pkg. (large size) frozen whole or sliced strawberries (no sugar added)*

Place pretzels and butter or margarine in bottom of a 9 × 13-inch baking dish and bake 10 minutes at 400 degrees. Cool. Cream cheese and sugar. Spread over top of lukewarm baked pretzels. Spread whipped topping on top of cheese and chill. Dissolve gelatin in boiling pineapple juice or water. Stir in strawberries and allow to thicken almost to jelled point. Spread over topping and refrigerate.

STRAWBERRY TACO SALAD

4 oz. tortilla chips
2 cups shredded lettuce
1 cup sour cream
2 avocados
1 tbsp. lemon juice
¼ tsp. salt
2 cups strawberries, halved
½ cup shredded cheddar cheese

Serve as one large or four individual salads. Place tortilla chips on bottom of plate and sprinkle them with shredded lettuce. Spoon sour cream over the lettuce and then spoon on avocado which has been mashed with lemon juice and salt. Add strawberries and sprinkle shredded cheese on top. Serves 4.

STRAWBERRY FRUIT SALAD

2 cans (11 oz.) Mandarin oranges, drained
6 medium-sized bananas, sliced
1 No. 2 can crushed pineapple, drained
1 pkg. (6 oz.) miniature marshmallows
2 eggs, beaten
1 cup sugar
1 tbsp. flour
1 pkg. (3 oz.) strawberry gelatin

Combine pineapple juice, eggs, sugar, and flour. Cook over low heat until thick (about 5 minutes). Add gelatin, stirring until dissolved. Cool before adding the fruit and marshmallows. Chill several hours. Serves 12.

FRESH FRUIT ELEGANCE

1 fresh pineapple, chilled
2 bananas, sliced
1 cup strawberries, chilled
½ cup blueberries, chilled
½ cup lime sherbet
½ cup mayonnaise

Keeping the crown intact, carefully cut the pineapple to resemble a basket with a handle. Scoop out fruit. Discard the core and cut pineapple into cubes. Combine pineapple, bananas, and strawberries and place in pineapple basket shell. Just before serving, sprinkle with blueberries. Combine sherbet and mayonnaise. Chill. Serve over fruit salad.

FRESH FRUIT AND YOGURT SALAD

3 cups strawberries
1 cantaloupe, cut in pieces
3 peaches, sliced
2 bananas, sliced
1 cup white seedless grapes
½ cup shredded coconut
2 cups yogurt
¼ cup honey
2 tsp. vanilla
¼ cup sunflower seeds

Combine fruits and coconut. In a blender combine yogurt, honey, and vanilla and blend. Carefully fold yogurt mixture into the fruit. Garnish with sunflower seeds. Serves 6.

FRUIT AND NUT SALAD

3 cups strawberries or raspberries
1 cup blueberries
2 cups thin slices of orange
1 cup coarsely chopped nuts
1½ cups yogurt
⅓ cup orange juice
2 tbsp. honey
Salad greens

Combine fruit and nuts. Combine yogurt, orange juice, and honey and fold into fruit on salad greens. Serves 6–8.

HONEYDEW AND BERRY SALAD

1 honeydew melon
Salad greens
¼ tsp. ground ginger
1 cup strawberries
½ cup raspberries
4 green grape clusters

Place honeydew wedges on salad greens of your choice. Sprinkle with ground ginger. Top with strawberries, raspberries, and green grape clusters. The green grape clusters may be frosted by dipping them in beaten egg white and then in sugar. Serve with your favorite dressing. Serves 4.

STRAWBERRY MELON SALAD BOWL

1 pint strawberries, hulled and cored
1 cantaloupe
½ honeydew melon
½ clove garlic
Lettuce
Lime French dressing (or lemon mayonnaise dressing)

All melons should be served very cold. The melon pulp may be shaped into balls, or diced, or scooped out in large spoonfuls. Rub a bowl with garlic and line with lettuce leaves. Arrange the strawberries and melon balls on lettuce and serve with dressing. Serves 6.

FROZEN SUMMER FRUIT SALAD

½ cup strawberries, hulled, cored, and sliced
½ cup diced canned pineapple
½ cup diced orange segments
½ cup diced bananas
2 tsp. lemon juice
1 tsp. unflavored gelatin
1 tbsp. cold water
4 tsp. strained honey
⅔ cup heavy cream, whipped
Lettuce

Strawberry Glazed
Cheese Cake

Chocolate-Dipped
Strawberries

Strawberry Crepes

Dessert Pizza
with Fresh Fruit

Chocolate-Painted
Strawberry Fans

Strawberry Cheese Pie

American Flag
Shortcake

Strawberry Tarts

Combine the fruits with lemon juice. Chill. Soften the gelatin in cold water. Dissolve over hot water and add to honey and fruit. Fold whipped cream into the fruit mixture and freeze in refrigerator tray 3 hours or until firm. Cut into squares and serve on lettuce. Serves 8.

Note: This salad may also be frozen in a round can of desired size and then sliced and served.

STRAWBERRY CREAM SALAD DRESSING

1 cup mashed fresh strawberries
⅓ tbsp. confectioners' sugar
3 tbsp. lemon juice
1 cup heavy cream, whipped

Combine first three ingredients and fold in the whipped cream.

DELICIOUS FRUIT SALAD

16 large marshmallows
1 cup milk
1 pkg. (3 oz.) lime gelatin
1 pkg. (6 oz.) cream cheese
1 can (14 oz.) pineapple, crushed style, drained
¾ cup juice from pineapple
½ cup mayonnaise
3 cups whole frozen strawberries, thawed and drained
¾ cup juice from strawberries (including water if needed)
1 pkg. (3 oz.) strawberry gelatin
1 cup cold water

In a double boiler, melt the marshmallows in the milk. Add lime gelatin and stir until dissolved. Add cream cheese and pineapple juice and mix. Chill until the mixture starts to thicken, then fold in pineapple and mayonnaise. Pour into a 2-quart dish. Refrigerate. For the second layer, bring strawberry juice to a boil. Add gelatin and stir to dissolve. Add cold water. Chill until mixture thickens. Fold in strawberries. Carefully pour over the first layer. Refrigerate. Serves 12.

STRAWBERRY AND BLUE CHEESE SALAD

First layer:

1 tbsp. gelatin
¼ cup cold water
2 cups cottage cheese, drained
½ cup liquid from cottage cheese (including milk if needed)
2 tbsp. blue cheese

Soften gelatin in the cold water, then dissolve over hot water. Combine cottage cheese, milk, and blue cheese and blend well. Add gelatin mixture and blend. Pour into a 2-quart dish or mold. Refrigerate until almost set.

Second layer:

2 cups frozen unsweetened sliced strawberries, thawed and drained
1 cup juice from strawberries (including water if needed)
¾ cup cold water
1 pkg. (3 oz.) strawberry gelatin

Heat to boiling the one cup of juice to dissolve gelatin. Add cold water and chill until mixture thickens. Fold in strawberries. Carefully pour over top of salad. Refrigerate until firm. Serves 6–8.

STRAWBERRY PIZZA

1 loaf frozen white bread dough, thawed and cut in half crosswise
1 pound cream cheese
½ cup sugar
6 tbsp. flour
2 egg yolks
2 tsp. fresh lemon juice
1 tsp. grated lemon peel
⅓ cup homemade strawberry jam, divided*
2 tbsp. sliced toasted almonds
2 cups halved fresh strawberries

Place each half of dough on greased baking sheet or pizza pan. Cover with greased foil and towel and let rise until double. Pat each half into a 12-inch circle, each about ¼-inch thick. In mixing bowl, place cream cheese, sugar, flour, egg yolks, lemon juice and peel and beat until smooth. Spread each circle of dough with half the cheese mixture to within ½ inch of edge. Cover loosely with greased foil and a towel. Let rise 45 minutes.

Bake in preheated oven 375 degrees for 20–25 minutes, until lightly browned. Remove from oven. Spread each pizza with strawberry jam and sprinkle with almonds. Bake 5 minutes longer. Serve hot.

For extra flavor place halved fresh strawberries on hot jam topping and serve. Leftover pizza wedges are good heated in a toaster oven. Yields two 12-inch pizzas.

*See recipes for jam in Part 5.

PIZZA CRUST

1 cup flour
1 tbsp. baking powder
½ tsp. salt
2 tbsp. vegetable oil
½ cup milk

Preheat oven to 375 degrees. Sift flour, baking powder, and salt together. Combine vegetable oil and milk and add to dry ingredients. Knead about 20 times. Press into lightly oiled pizza pan. Cover with choice of toppings. Bake 15–20 minutes. Yields one 12-inch pizza.

WHOLE WHEAT PIZZA CRUST

1 tsp. Fermipan yeast (instant yeast)
½ cup lukewarm water
1 tbsp. vegetable oil
¾ cup whole wheat flour
¼ cup white flour

Preheat oven to 375 degrees. In a medium-sized bowl, combine the yeast and lukewarm water. Add oil and whole wheat and white flours. Knead until dough is soft. Let rise 5 minutes. Spread on lightly oiled pizza pan. Cover with choice of toppings. Bake 25–30 minutes. Yields one 12-inch pizza.

PIZZA TOPPING I

Frozen strawberries, thawed and drained, with water to yield ½ cup
½ cup jellied cranberry sauce
1 cup shredded mozzarella cheese

Preheat oven to 375 degrees. Combine strawberries and cranberry sauce. Spread over pizza base. Sprinkle with shredded mozzarella cheese. Bake about 15–20 minutes.

PIZZA TOPPING II

1 cup strawberry jam
1 cup shredded Velveeta cheese

Preheat oven to 375 degrees. Spread pizza base with strawberry jam. Sprinkle shredded Velveeta cheese on top. Bake about 15–20 minutes.

PIZZA TOPPING III

1 cup cottage cheese
1 tbsp. sour cream
1 egg yolk
¾ cup strawberry or raspberry jam

Preheat oven to 375 degrees. Combine cottage cheese, sour cream, and egg yolk. Spread over pizza crust. Spread jam on top. Bake about 15–20 minutes.

PIZZA TOPPING IV

1 cup strawberry jam or 1 cup raspberry jam
1 tbsp. grated crystallized ginger
1 cup shredded mozzarella cheese
¾ cup chopped nuts

Preheat oven to 375 degrees. Combine jam and grated ginger. Spread over pizza crust. Sprinkle shredded mozzarella cheese over jam. Sprinkle nuts over the cheese. Bake about 15–20 minutes.

DESSERT PIZZA WITH FRESH FRUIT

Crust:

1½ tsp. Fermipan yeast (instant yeast)
½ cup milk, warm
2 tsp. sugar
½ tsp. salt
1 tbsp. butter
1 egg, slightly beaten
1⅓ cups flour

Cheese topping:

1 pkg. (8 oz.) cream cheese
¼ cup sugar
1 egg yolk
1 tbsp. grated ginger
2 tbsp. flour
⅛ tsp. cardamon
⅛ tsp. mace

Fruit topping:

2 cups strawberry halves
2–3 bananas, sliced
4 kiwi fruit, sliced
½ cup currant jelly, raspberry or strawberry, melted

Add yeast to warm milk. Add sugar, salt, butter, and beaten egg. Mix in flour. Knead 10 times. Grease a medium-sized bowl. Add dough to bowl and turn the dough to coat all surfaces. Cover with a towel and let rise in warm area until double in volume, about 45 minutes. Press into a 12-inch pizza pan.

Preheat oven to 350 degrees. Beat cheese topping ingredients together. Spread over pizza crust. Bake about 20 minutes until browned and until cheese topping is set. Cool. Decorate the top with fruit. Brush with the melted jelly. Serves 8.

Note: Other fruit combinations may be used for topping.

4. FRUITS, YOGURTS, DESSERTS

Give no more to all your guests,
Than they are able to digest.
Give them always of the prime,
And but little at a time.

FRESH PINEAPPLE AND STRAWBERRY SUPREME

Pare one small ripe pineapple and slice thinly. Cut into wedges. Marinate wedges in dry white wine. Refrigerate. Arrange undrained pineapple wedges in sherbet glasses or fruit sauces. Pour a little more wine over each and garnish with fresh strawberries.

STRAWBERRY-BANANA DELIGHT

2 pkgs. (3 oz.) strawberry gelatin
2 pkgs. (10 oz.) frozen strawberries
1 small can drained crushed pineapple
3 mashed bananas
1 box Dream Whip or other dessert topping

Prepare gelatin with 2 cups boiling water. Add frozen strawberries, drained pineapple, and mashed bananas. Pour *half* into bowl and let set. Put layer of Dream Whip or other topping on top of set strawberry gelatin and pour remaining strawberry mixture on top to form another layer, finishing with rest of dessert topping.

STEWED RHUBARB, STRAWBERRIES, AND BANANAS

2 pounds rhubarb, trimmed and cut into 1-inch pieces
¾ cup sugar, or less
1 cup strawberries, hulled, cored, and sliced
1–2 medium bananas, peeled and sliced
Sour cream (optional)

Simmer rhubarb and sugar in a saucepan for 12–15 minutes. Remove from stove and add the strawberries and bananas. Mix well. Serve either warm or chilled. Put a tablespoon of sour cream on top of each serving if you like. Serves 4–6.

STRAWBERRY-FILLED MELON

2 small cantaloupes
1 tbsp. cornstarch
1 tbsp. water
1 pkg. (16 oz.) frozen strawberries or raspberries
½ cup red currant jelly
1 small sprig fresh mint
Few grains salt

In a saucepan, stir cornstarch into water and add berries, jelly, and mint. Bring to a boil, lower heat, and simmer 5 minutes. Remove mint. Press berries through a sieve and discard seeds. Chill. Cut the cantaloupes in half and remove seeds. Cut a thin slice from the bottom of the melons so they sit flat. Using a melon ball cutter, scoop balls from the rim of the melon, and pile them in the center of melon half. Fill holes and center with sauce.

FRUIT-TOPPED CANAPES

1 pkg. (8 oz.) cream cheese, softened
1 tsp. grated orange rind
½ tsp. ground ginger
48 multi-shaped crackers, lightly toasted
8 fresh strawberries
½ cup fresh blueberries
¼ medium honeydew melon
¾ cup red grapes
¾ cup green grapes
½ cup fresh pineapple wedges, drained
1 or 2 kiwi
Small fresh mint leaves

Beat cream cheese until smooth. Add orange rind, orange juice, and ginger, mixing well. Spoon into a pastry bag and pipe the mixture onto crackers. Set aside. Cut fruit into various shapes and place on crackers, decorating tops as desired with fruit and mint leaves. Yields 48 canapes.

STRAWBERRY-RASPBERRIES AMBROSIA

1 pkg. (10 oz.) frozen strawberries
1 pkg. (10 oz.) frozen raspberries
1 lb. seedless grapes or ½ pound Malaga grapes, halved
2 cups flaked coconut
½ to 1 pint commercial sour cream
Confectioners' sugar (optional)

Combine thawed berries, adding grapes, coconut, sour cream, and sugar mixture if not sweet enough. Toss lightly to mix. Serve buffet style in a decorative bowl with small dabs of sour cream and sprinkling of coconut, or spoon into individual sherbet glasses.

STRAWBERRY AND FRUIT KABOBS

Bamboo skewers as required. Arrange unblemished strawberries alternately on skewers with cubed pineapple, watermelon, honeydew melon, and grapes of desired color. Cubes of cheese may also be included. Remember to leave ¾-inch free at the bottom, to use as a holder. Strive to make the size of melon cubes as uniform as possible. Alternate colors for festive effect. Arrange on serving platter in desired pattern.

STRAWBERRIES AND STARFRUIT IN CHAMPAGNE

2 cups strawberries, hulled, cored, and cut in half
2 starfruit
½ cup sugar
¼ cup champagne or catawba juice

Cut starfruit crosswise into ¼-inch slices. Sprinkle with sugar and let stand 30 minutes. Spoon starfruit and prepared strawberries into dessert dishes. Pour champagne over fruit.

STRAWBERRY-RASPBERRY SUPREME

1 pint strawberries, washed, stemmed, cored, and lightly sugared
1 pkg. (16 oz.) frozen raspberries

When raspberries are still slightly crystallized, work through sieve to remove seeds or first blend in blender. Spoon strawberries into serving dishes. Pour the raspberry puree over the top and chill. Serve with whipped cream.

STRAWBERRIES AND PINEAPPLE WITH KIRSCH

1½ cups strawberries, hulled and cored
1½ cups fresh diced pineapple
½ cup sugar
½ cup water
2 tbsp. kirsch

Mix fruit, put into a serving bowl, and chill. Combine sugar and water, bring to a boil, and simmer for 5 minutes. Chill. About 1 hour before serving, add kirsch to the syrup. Pour it over the fruit and garnish with fresh mint leaves. Serves 4.

RAINBOW FRUIT DESSERT

1 large mango (about one pound), peeled
2 cups fresh blueberries
2 bananas, sliced
2 cups fresh strawberries, halved
2 cups seedless green grapes
2 nectarines, unpeeled and sliced
1 kiwi, peeled and sliced
Honey-orange sauce

Layer fruit in order listed in a serving bowl. Just before serving, pour on honey-orange sauce. Yields 12 servings (about 102 calories per 1-cup serving).

Honey-Orange Sauce:

⅓ *cup unsweetened orange juice*
2 *tbsp. lemon juice*
1½ *tbsp. honey*
¼ *tsp. ground ginger*
Dash of ground nutmeg

Combine all ingredients in a bowl and mix well. Yields ½ cup.

STRAWBERRY YOGURT DELIGHT

1 *can (8 oz.) unsweetened crushed pineapple*
1 *envelope unflavored gelatin*
1 *pkg. (10 oz.) frozen strawberries, thawed*
1 *carton (8 oz.) strawberry low-fat yogurt*
1 *tsp. grated lemon rind*
Whipped topping (optional)
Lemon wedges (optional)

Drain pineapple, reserving juice. Sprinkle gelatin over pineapple juice and let stand 1 minute. Stir mixture over low heat 2–3 minutes or until gelatin dissolves. Remove from heat. Add strawberries, pineapple, yogurt, and lemon rind. Mix well. Pour into six dessert dishes and chill thoroughly. Garnish each serving with whipped topping and lemon wedge if desired. Serves 6.

STRAWBERRY YOGURT WHIP

1 *pkg. (3 oz.) strawberry gelatin*
1 *cup boiling water*
¾ *cup cold water*
1 *carton (8 oz.) strawberry yogurt*

Dissolve gelatin in boiling water. Add cold water. Chill until slightly thickened. Add yogurt and beat with rotary beater until mixture is light and fluffy. Pour into punch cups or individual serving dishes. Chill about 2 hours. Makes 4 cups or 8 servings.

STRAWBERRY CROWN

1 envelope unflavored gelatin
½ cup cold water
2 envelopes low-calorie strawberry gelatin
2½ cups hot water
2 cups (1 pint) strawberries
1 carton (8 oz.) vanilla flavored yogurt

Soften unflavored gelatin in cold water in a small saucepan. Heat, stirring constantly, just until gelatin dissolves. Remove from heat. Dissolve strawberry gelatin in hot water in a medium-sized bowl. Stir in the plain gelatin mixture and pour ½ cup into a 6-cup mold. Chill 15 minutes or just until syrupy. Let remaining gelatin stand at room temperature to cool. Set aside 12 whole strawberries for garnish, then hull the remaining ones. Arrange 6 berries in a ring in gelatin in the mold. Spoon 2 tablespoons reserved gelatin mixture over the berries. In a bowl, beat yogurt into the gelatin mixture. Chill just until syrupy. Slice the remaining strawberries. Fold them into the yogurt mixture and spoon over the sticky-firm layer in mold. Chill until firm. When ready to serve run a sharp-tipped, thin-bladed knife around the top of mold. Dip mold very quickly in and out of a pan of hot water. Cover mold with a serving plate, turn upside down, then gently lift off mold. Garnish with whole strawberries. Serves 6.

STRAWBERRY DESSERT I

½ cup butter or margarine, softened
1 cup flour
½ cup brown sugar
½ cup chopped pecans
20 large marshmallows
1 pkg. strawberries (10 oz.)
1 cup whipping cream or dessert topping

Mix ½ cup butter with flour. Add brown sugar and chopped pecans. Spread mixture in an 8 × 8-inch pan and bake 15 minutes at 400 degrees. Remove from oven, stir with a fork, and crumble. Put this mixture in an 8 × 8-inch pan, saving some for topping. In a double boiler melt marshmallows with the juice drained from strawberries and cool. Add berries and 1 cup whipped cream and spread over crumbs. Put rest of crumbs on top. Chill before serving.

STRAWBERRY DESSERT II

Crust:

1 cup flour
¼ cup brown sugar
¾ cup chopped nuts
½ cup butter or margarine

Fillng:

30 marshmallows
⅔ cup milk
1 cup whipping cream
2 boxes (3 oz. ea.) strawberry gelatin
2 cups hot water
2 pkgs. (10 oz. ea.) frozen strawberries

Mix flour, sugar, and butter and then add nuts. Pat in 9 × 13-inch baking pan. Bake 15 minutes at 350 degrees. Cool. Melt marshmallows in milk over heat, stirring constantly. Cool. Fold in the cream after whipping it. Spread over the crust and refrigerate until set. Dissolve gelatin in hot water and immediately stir in the frozen berries. Chill until it starts to congeal, then spoon over marshmallow layer. Chill.

STRAWBERRY DESSERT III

1 pint frozen strawberries, thawed
1 pkg. (3 oz.) strawberry gelatin
1 cup boiling water
1 store-bought angel food cake
Whipping cream

Mix gelatin and boiling water and cool until jelled. Break up an angel food cake over the bottom of an 8 × 8-inch dish or pan. Whip ½ pint whipping cream. Mix strawberries into gelatin and fold in whipped cream. Pour over angel food cake and mix. Let set overnight. Note: Freezing cake pieces before mixing with gelatin-strawberry mixture prevents loss of volume.

STRAWBERRY DESSERT IV

2 boxes (3 oz. ea.) strawberry gelatin
2 cups boiling water
2 pkgs. (10 oz.) frozen strawberries
1 can (large) crushed pineapple
2 bananas, mashed
1 carton sour cream

Dissolve gelatin and while still hot, add frozen strawberries, pineapple, and mashed bananas. Pour ½ mixture into pan and let set. Spread sour cream on top and remainder of gelatin mixture. Chill until firm.

STRAWBERRY HEART

1 pkg. (10 oz.) frozen sliced strawberries, thawed
1 pkg. (3 oz.) strawberry gelatin
6 tbsp. lemon juice
½ cup instant nonfat dry milk powder
½ cup ice water
¼ cup flaked coconut

Drain strawberries, reserving syrup. Add enough water to syrup to make one cup liquid. Heat to boiling point. Add gelatin. Stir until dissolved. Add 4 tablespoons of the lemon juice and strawberries. Mix well. Chill until slightly thickened. Beat until light and fluffy. Combine dry milk powder with ice water in a bowl. Beat until soft peaks form (3–4 minutes). Add remaining lemon juice. Continue beating until stiff peaks form (3–4 minutes longer). Fold whipped milk and coconut into strawberry mixture. Pour into a 1-quart mold. Chill until firm. Unmold and serve with additional thawed frozen strawberries, if desired. Serves 8.

STRAWBERRY FLUFF
(43 calories per serving)

2 pkgs. strawberry low-calorie gelatin
½ cup hot water
½ cup crushed fresh strawberries
¾ cup well-chilled evaporated milk

Dissolve gelatin in very hot water. Chill until it begins to thicken. Add crushed strawberries. Whip the evaporated milk until almost stiff and fold into the gelatin mixture. Pour into dessert glasses. Chill until firm. Serves 4.

STRAWBERRY SPONGE

1 envelope unflavored gelatin
½ cup cold water
1 tbsp. liquid sweetener
1 tbsp. lemon juice
1 pint frozen strawberries
2 egg whites

Soften gelatin in cold water in the top of a double boiler. Add sweetener and lemon juice. Stir constantly over hot water until gelatin is dissolved. Remove from heat and add crushed strawberries. Let stand until light and fluffy. Beat egg whites until stiff, then fold into gelatin mixture. Spoon into 6 individual molds or a 1½-quart mold. Chill until firm. Serves 6.

STRAWBERRIES TO DIP

Wash 1 pint fresh unblemished strawberries; do not hull. Chill. To serve, divide berries among individual serving dishes. Pass bowls of sour cream and brown sugar to be spooned onto dishes. Berries are first dipped into sour cream, then into sugar. Serves 4.

STRAWBERRY WAFFLES À LA MODE

1 pint fresh strawberries, hulled, cored, and sliced
2 frozen small waffles, about 3 inches square
Vanilla ice cream

Heat frozen waffles until crisp. Place scoop of ice cream on each waffle and top with strawberries that have been sweetened to taste. Serves 2.

STRAWBERRY BONANZA

4 cups biscuit mix
Sugar
½ cup melted butter or margarine
1 cup milk
2 pints fresh California strawberries, hulled, cored, and halved
Orange or lemon marmalade
1 pint sour cream

Blend biscuit mix, ¼ cup sugar, butter, and milk. Knead gently on lightly floured surface 8–10 times. Pat out ⅓ of the dough in each of three 9-inch layer cake pans. Bake in 450 degree oven for 12 minutes until lightly browned. Combine strawberries and ⅔ cup sugar. Chill for 30 minutes. Stack biscuit layers, spreading each thinly with marmalade and sour cream. Top with sliced strawberries.

FRESH STRAWBERRY TURNOVER

¼ cup sugar
1 tbsp. plus 1½ tsp. cornstarch
1 pint (2 cups) fresh strawberries, hulled and cored

Mix ingredients in a saucepan and cook over medium heat, stirring constantly, until mixture thickens and boils. Boil and stir 1 minute. Cool.

Heat oven to 425 degrees. Prepare pastry as follows:

1½ cups flour
½ tsp. salt
½ cup shortening
3–4 tbsp. cold water

Roll pastry into a 14-inch circle. Then fold it into quarters so it can be lifted and centered on an ungreased baking sheet. Spread strawberry filling on one half of circle to within 1½ inches of the edge. Folk the other half of pastry over filling, sealing edges. Turn up ½ inch of edge and flute. Cut slits in the top and bake until golden brown, about 35 minutes. Cool slightly and spread with frosty glaze.

Frosty Glaze:
½ cup confectioners' sugar
1 tbsp. butter or margarine, softened
1 tbsp. light cream
1 tsp. grated lemon peel

Mix all ingredients until smooth, and spread on turnover. Cut into wedges and serve warm. Serves 6.

STRAWBERRY JAM PUDDING
(a berry lover's dream)

1 cup butter, softened
1 cup strawberry jam
3 eggs, separated
½ cup plus 2 tbsp. flour
1 cup plus 1 tbsp. sugar
1 tsp. baking soda
3 tbsp. Buttermilk
1 tsp. vanilla
1 cup water

Combine ½ cup butter, jam, egg yolks, ½ cup flour, and one tablespoon sugar. Dissolve baking soda in buttermilk and stir into jam mixture. Fold in beaten egg whites. Pour into an 8 × 8-inch baking dish. Bake for about 45 minutes at 300–325 degrees. Blend remaining butter, flour, sugar, vanilla, and water. Cook until thickened. Serve over pudding. Yields 6–9 servings.

STRAWBERRIES WITH CHOCOLATE CREAM

1 cup whipping cream
3 tbsp. cocoa
¼ cup plus 1 tbsp. powdered sugar
2 qts. medium-sized fresh strawberries

Beat whipping cream until foamy. Sift cocoa and powdered sugar together. Add to cream, beating until soft peaks form. Serve with strawberries. Yields about 78 appetizers.

GRANNY'S COOKIES

1 cup lard
1 cup margarine
8 cups flour
¾ cup sugar
½ tsp. soda
1 tsp. baking powder
⅛ tsp. salt
3 eggs
1 cup evaporated milk
1 tbsp. lemon juice
1 cup strawberry or raspberry jam

Preheat oven to 350 degrees. Combine lard, margarine, flour, sugar, soda, baking powder, and salt, as for pie dough. Stir in eggs, milk, and lemon juice. Roll out and cut with favorite cookie cutter. Bake about 10 minutes. Cool. Spread one cookie with jam and top with another cookie. These cookies seem best the second day after they absorb the jam. They can be cut with a large cutter for the "king-sized" appetite. Yields 48 sandwich cookies.

STRAWBERRY SUPREME

2 pkgs. (3 oz.) or 1 pkg. (6 oz.) strawberry gelatin
¼ tsp. salt
2 cups boiling water
1½ cups cold water
1 pkg. (10 oz.) frozen strawberries
1 cup softened vanilla ice cream or sour cream
1½ tbsp. brandy
1½ tbsp. rum
2 tbsp. Cointreau liqueur

Dissolve gelatin and salt in boiling water. Add cold water. Measure 2 cups into a separate bowl. Add the frozen fruit. Stir carefully until fruit thaws and separates. Chill until mixture is almost set (about 15 minutes). Spoon into sherbet glasses, filling each about ⅔ full. Chill until set but not firm.

Chill remaining gelatin until slightly thickened. Blend in ice cream, brandy, rum, and liqueur. Beat one minute or until bubbly. Spoon over gelatin in glasses. Chill until firm, about 3 hours. Makes 5½ cups or 10 servings.

FESTIVE STRAWBERRY DESSERTS

Meringue Shells:

2 egg whites
⅛ tsp. cream of tartar
Dash salt
½ cup sugar
½ tsp. vanilla
Dessert topping or whipped cream

Beat egg whites with cream of tartar and salt until stiff but not dry. Add sugar, 1 tablespoon at a time, beating until stiff after each addition. Fold in vanilla. Heap in rounds (or other desired shape for special occasions) onto baking sheet covered with heavy ungreased paper. Using back of tablespoon, hollow out a depression in the center. Bake in slow oven (275 degrees) 40–60 minutes or until lightly browned. Remove at once from paper. Cool. Makes 18 large meringues.

Fill shells with desired amount of fresh, unblemished strawberries that have been cored and sweetened to taste. Strawberries may be cut in half for easier eating if desired. Decorate with dollop of whipped topping and a strawberry. If preferred, a dish of topping may be passed so guests may serve themselves.

STRAWBERRY DELIGHT

2½ cups crushed graham crackers
½ cup sugar
⅔ cup butter or margarine, melted
2 small boxes frozen strawberries
2 pkgs. (3 oz. ea.) strawberry gelatin
2 cups boiling water
1 pkg. (12 oz.) cream cheese, room temperature
1 carton (9 oz.) whipped topping
½ cup chopped walnuts
2 cups powdered sugar

Mix graham cracker crumbs, sugar, and melted butter or margarine together. Press into 9 × 13-inch pan to form crust. Mix gelatin, boiling water, and strawberries. Set aside. Combine cream cheese, whipped topping, walnuts, and powdered sugar. Pour into crumb crust. After strawberry mixture has thickened, pour over cream cheese layer to make top layer. Note: 1 cup boiling water may be used instead of 2 to set gelatin faster.

STRAWBERRY SNOWCAP

½ cup butter or margarine, softened
¼ cup brown sugar (packed)
1 cup flour
½ cup chopped pecans
3 egg whites
¼ tsp. cream of tartar
¾ cup granulated sugar
½ tsp. vanilla
2 cups fresh strawberries, hulled and cored
½ cup granulated sugar
1 quart strawberry ice cream

Heat oven to 400 degrees. Mix butter, brown sugar, flour and pecans. Press mixture evenly in ungreased pan 9 × 9 × 2 inches. Beat egg whites and cream of tartar until foamy. Beat in ¾ cup granulated sugar, 1 tablespoon at a time; continue beating until stiff and glossy. Fold in vanilla and crumb mixture. Pour into pan. Bake until light brown, about 35 minutes. Cool.

Sprinkle strawberries with ½ cup granulated sugar; let stand 1 hour. Cut meringue into wedges. Serve with scoops of ice cream topped with strawberries. Serves 6–8.

HELEN'S 20's STRAWBERRY DESSERT

Crust:

½ cup margarine or butter
¼ cup brown sugar
½ cup chopped nuts
1 cup flour

Mix together and bake on a large cookie sheet at 350 degrees for 10 minutes. Partially cool and break with fork into crumbs. Place *one half* of the crumb mixture in a 9 × 13-inch pan.

Filling:

3 egg whites
⅔ cup sugar
1 pkg. (10 oz.) frozen strawberries
2 tsp. lemon juice
½ tsp. strawberry flavoring
1 pkg. Dream Whip or other dessert topping

Beat egg whites until stiff and fold in sugar gradually as you continue beating. Fold in thawed strawberries, lemon juice, and strawberry flavoring. Prepare Dream Whip according to directions and fold into strawberry mixture. Pour filling over crumbs and then top with the remainder of crumb mixture. Chill 6 hours or overnight.

STRAWBERRY-ORANGE CREAM

1½ pints strawberries, hulled and cored
¾ cup sugar
¾ cup fresh orange juice
3 tsp. grated orange rind
1½ tsp. lemon juice
1½ cups heavy cream, whipped

Drain strawberries on paper towels. Place in bowl and sprinkle with 1 tablespoon of sugar. Mix and let stand 30 minutes. Place remaining sugar, orange juice, rind, and lemon juice in a small saucepan. Bring to a boil. Stir and cook gently for 10 minutes. Remove from heat and cool. Combine whipped cream and cooled orange syrup. Spoon over berries and refrigerate until well chilled.

STRAWBERRIES WITH "CLOTTED" CREAM

Unblemished whole strawberries
1 pkg. (3 oz.) cream cheese, softened
1 tbsp. granulated sugar
Pinch salt
1 cup heavy cream

Mix the cheese with the sugar and salt until smooth. Stir in the cream and then whip until stiff. This makes 2 cups. Place small amounts on individual dessert plates surrounded with whole strawberries. Serve with a few Melba rounds. Guests serve themselves by dipping strawberries into the cream.

STRAWBERRY MOUSSELINE

3 pints fresh strawberries, hulled and cored
⅔ cup sugar
2 tbsp. rum
1 tbsp. lemon juice
1 tsp. vanilla
2 envelopes (2 tbsp.) unflavored gelatin
½ cup water
10–12 ladyfingers
½ cup curacao liqueur
1½ cups heavy cream, whipped
Additional strawberries for garnish

Run strawberries through a sieve or puree in blender with sugar, rum, lemon juice, and vanilla. Set aside in a bowl. Sprinkle gelatin over the surface of cold water and let soak until translucent, about 3 minutes, then heat in a saucepan until thoroughly dissolved. Add to pureed strawberries. Set the bowl into a larger bowl filled with cracked ice and stir mixture until it begins to thicken.

Rinse a mold (fluted) with cold water. Sprinkle ladyfingers with curacao and line the sides of the mold with them. Fold the whipped cream into the berry mixture and pour into mold. Refrigerate for several hours or overnight until firm and well chilled. Loosen the edges and sides with a spatula (use a warm, damp cloth, if necessary). Unmold on serving dish and garnish with whole unblemished strawberries.

STRAWBERRY ON A CLOUD

6 egg whites
½ tsp. cream of tartar
¼ tsp. salt
1¾ cups sugar
2 pkgs. (3 oz. ea.) cream cheese, softened
1 cup sugar
1 tsp. vanilla
2 cups chilled whipping cream
2 cups miniature marshmallows
Strawberry topping (recipe below)

Heat oven to 375 degrees. Grease an oblong pan, 13 × 9 × 2 inches. Beat egg whites, cream of tartar, and salt until foamy. Beat in the 1¾ cups sugar, one tablespoon at a time, and continue beating until stiff and glossy. Do not underbeat. Spread in pan. Bake one hour. Turn off the oven and leave the meringue inside with the oven door closed, about 12 hours. Blend the cream cheese, one cup sugar, and the vanilla. In a chilled bowl, beat the whipping cream until stiff. Gently fold whipped cream and marshmallows into cream cheese mixture. Spread over meringue. Refrigerate 12–24 hours. Serve with strawberry topping (below). Serves 10–12.

Strawberry topping:

Stir together one can (21 ounces) cherry pie filling, one teaspoon lemon juice, and 2 cups sliced fresh strawberries or one package (16 ounces) frozen strawberries, thawed.

STRAWBERRIES ROMANOFF I

1 quart strawberries, hulled, cored, and cut in half
½ cup powdered sugar
3–4 tbsp. kirsch or orange-flavored liqueur
1 cup whipping cream

Reserve 6 strawberry halves for garnish. Sprinkle remaining halves with powdered sugar and kirsch and lightly toss. Cover and refrigerate 2 hours. Just before serving, beat whipping cream until soft peaks form. Fold in strawberries. Garnish each serving with reserved berry half.

STRAWBERRIES ROMANOFF II

1 pint strawberries, fresh or partially frozen
1 cup orange juice
¼ cup curacao or Grand Marnier
1 pint vanilla ice cream

Pour orange juice over berries and let steep at least 30 minutes in refrigerator. Stir in liqueur. Serve ice cream on chilled plates and top with flavored strawberries.

STRAWBERRIES ROMANOFF III

1 pint strawberries, washed, stemmed, and cored
2 tbsp. sugar
2 pkgs. (3 oz. ea.) or one 6-oz. pkg. strawberry gelatin
2 cups boiling water
2 tbsp. brandy (or ½ tsp. brandy extract and 3 tbsp. orange juice)
1 tbsp. Cointreau or curacao liqueur
2 cups whipped topping

Set aside a few whole berries for garnish if desired. Slice remaining berries. Add sugar and let stand 15 minutes. Drain berries, measuring syrup. Add water to syrup to make one cup. Dissolve gelatin in boiling water. Measure ¾ cup of the gelatin; add brandy liqueur and ½ cup of the measured liquid. Chill until slightly thickened. Fold in whipped topping. Pour into a 5- or 6-cup mold. Chill until set but not firm. Add remaining ½ cup measured liquid to remaining gelatin. Chill until thickened. Stir in strawberries. Spoon into mold. Chill until firm, about 4 hours or overnight. Unmold and garnish with berries. Makes 6 cups or 8–10 servings.

SOUTHAMPTON STRAWBERRIES
(A Takeoff on Strawberries Romanoff)

2 pints (2 pounds) fresh strawberries
3 tbsp. granulated sugar
4 tbsp. cognac
3 tbsp. Grand Marnier

1 cup heavy cream
½ tsp. vanilla extract
1 cup vanilla ice cream

Wash, hull, and core strawberries. Drain on paper towels. About 3 hours before serving time, slice each berry in two or three and place in a bowl with 2 tablespoons of sugar (reserving 1 tablespoon), 3 tablespoons cognac (reserving 1 tablespoon), and the Grand Marnier. Mix gently. Cover with plastic wrap and refrigerate.

Whip cream with the vanilla and the reserved tablespoons of sugar and cognac, whipping only until the mixture holds its shape. Refrigerate.

About a half hour before serving, place ice cream in the refrigerator to soften a bit. Just before serving, mix ice cream and berries (only slightly) and place in a chilled serving bowl. Pour whipped cream over berries and ice cream. Serve in shallow dessert bowls which have been chilled. Serves 6.

BERRIES IN A CLOUD

For convenience, make the meringue shell a day before serving. Fill within 2 hours of serving.

3 egg whites
1 tsp. vanilla
¼ tsp. cream of tartar
1 cup sugar
½ cup finely chopped toasted almonds

1 pkg. (3 oz.) cream cheese, softened
½ cup packed brown sugar
½ cup unsweetened cocoa powder

2 tbsp. milk
½ tsp. vanilla
1 cup whipping cream

3 cups fresh whole strawberries, stems and caps removed
2 sq. (2 oz.) semisweet chocolate, cut up
2 tsp. shortening

Let egg whites stand at room temperature for 30 minutes. Cover a baking sheet with plain brown paper or parchment paper. Draw a 9-inch circle on the paper. Set aside.

In a large mixing bowl combine egg whites, the teaspoon of vanilla, and cream of tartar. Beat with an electric mixer on medium speed until soft peaks form. Gradually add the sugar, one tablespoon at a time, beating on high speed until very stiff peaks form (tips stand straight) and sugar is almost dissolved. Fold in the chopped almonds. Spread meringue mixture over the circle drawn on paper, building the sides up taller than the center to form a shell. Bake in a 300-degree oven for 45 minutes. Turn off the oven and let meringue dry with oven door closed at least one hour (do not open door). Remove baking sheet from oven. Lift meringue and carefully peel off paper; transfer to a flat serving platter. (Or, store shell in a flat, airtight container overnight.)

For cocoa mousse, in a small mixing bowl beat cream cheese and brown sugar until smooth. Add cocoa powder, milk, and the ½ teaspoon vanilla. Beat until smooth. In another small chilled mixing bowl, beat whipping cream with chilled beaters of an electric mixer on medium speed to soft peaks. Fold into the cocoa mixture. Carefully spoon cocoa mousse into the meringue shell. Press whole berries, seam side down, into the mousse. In a small heavy saucepan melt semisweet chocolate and shortening over low heat, stirring constantly. With a small spoon, lightly drizzle over filling and meringue. Serve immediately, or cover and chill filled meringue for up to 2 hours. To serve, cut into wedges, dipping knife in water between cuts. Serves 10.

RUSSIAN CREAM WITH STRAWBERRIES ROMANOFF

Russian cream:

1 cup heavy cream
½ cup sugar
1 tbsp. gelatin
1 cup sour cream
½ tsp. vanilla

In saucepan mix together the heavy cream, sugar, and gelatin. Heat on low until the gelatin is dissolved. Cool until mixture slightly thickens. Fold in sour cream and vanilla. Cover and chill at least 4 hours.

Strawberries Romanoff:

4 cups fresh strawberries
½ cup confectioners' icing sugar
2 tbsp. vodka
2 tbsp. triple sec
2 tbsp. rum

Combine all ingredients and chill. At serving time spoon Russian Cream into your most beautiful dessert dishes. Top with strawberries Romanoff. Serves 4–6.

STRAWBERRY BAVARIAN CREAM I

4 cups strawberries, hulled and cored
1 tbsp. lemon juice
¾ cup sugar
2 envelopes gelatin
¼ cup water
2 cups heavy cream, whipped

Mash berries and put in blender to make puree. Add lemon juice and sugar to the strawberry puree and stir until the sugar is completely dissolved. Soften gelatin in water, then stir over hot water until dissolved. Fold dissolved gelatin into strawberry puree. Stir the puree over cracked ice until mixture begins to thicken. Fold in whipped cream. Pour into serving dish and chill. Serves 6.

STRAWBERRY BAVARIAN CREAM II

1 pkg. (10 oz.) frozen sliced strawberries, thawed
1 cup boiling water
1 pkg. (3 oz.) strawberry-flavored gelatin
1 cup whipping cream or dessert topping

Drain strawberries, reserving syrup. Pour boiling water over gelatin in a bowl and stir until dissolved. Add enough water to reserved strawberry syrup to make 1 cup and stir into dissolved gelatin. Chill until almost set. Beat gelatin mixture until foamy. Fold gelatin and strawberries into whipped cream and pour into individual molds, or a 1-quart mold. When firm, unmold and serve with more whipped cream, if desired. Serves 6–8.

STRAWBERRY BAVARIAN CREAM III

1 cup strawberry juice
1 envelope unflavored gelatin (1 tbsp.)
2 tbsp. cold water
½ cup sugar
¼ tsp. salt
1 cup crushed strawberries
1 tbsp. lemon juice
1 cup whipping cream, whipped stiff

Heat juice. Soften gelatin in cold water. Stir into hot strawberry juice. Stir in sugar and salt and blend in crushed strawberries and lemon juice. Cool. Stir occasionally until mixture is partially set. Beat with rotary beater. Fold in stiffly whipped cream. Pour into oiled 1-quart mold. Chill about 4 hours. Unmold on large serving dish. Garnish with colorful fresh fruits. Serves 8.

DELUXE BAVARIAN

1 raspberry jam-filled jelly roll
3 tbsp. gelatin
¾ cup cold water
6 cups fresh strawberries or 6 cups whole frozen strawberries, thawed and drained
2 tbsp. lemon juice
3 eggs
⅛ tsp. salt
1 cup sugar
2 cups whipping cream

Soften gelatin in cold water, then dissolve over hot water. Cool. Puree strawberries. Add lemon juice and gelatin. Beat eggs and salt until frothy. Add sugar gradually and beat until very light. Whip the cream until stiff. Fold strawberry and egg mixtures together. Fold in whipped cream. Line sides of a 10-inch springform pan with slices of jelly roll. Carefully pour strawberry mixture into pan. Refrigerate 8 hours or overnight. Serves 12.

STRAWBERRY CREAM IN MERINGUE SHELLS

6 egg whites, room temperature
1¼ tsp. salt
1½ tsp. cream of tartar
¾ cup sugar
1 quart strawberries
1 pint whipping cream
3 tbsp. Cointreau

Combine egg whites, salt, and cream of tartar. Beat until almost stiff. Gradually add sugar; beat until sugar is dissolved. Shape into cups on baking sheet, lined with ungreased heavy brown paper. Bake at 250 degrees for one hour. Turn off heat and cool meringues in the oven. Serve with crushed strawberries, sweetened whipped cream, and Cointreau. Serves 8.

STRAWBERRY AND COFFEE COUPE

Coupe (coop), a French word for fruit with ice cream, is an easy way to savor spring berries. This recipe features marinated berries over coffee ice cream that's swirled with sour cream.

82

1 pint coffee ice cream
1 cup dairy sour cream or plain yogurt
3 tbsp. coffee liqueur
2 cups sliced fresh strawberries (about 3 cups whole berries)
4–6 tsp. sugar (to taste)

In a medium bowl, stir ice cream with a spoon to soften. Stir in sour cream or yogurt and 2 tablespoons of the liqueur. Cover and return to freezer for 4–5 hours, or until firm. In a small bowl combine strawberries, sugar, and the remaining one tablespoon of liqueur. Cover and chill for at least 2 hours. To serve, scoop ice cream into dishes or goblets. Top with strawberries. Serves 4.

STRAWBERRY CHEESE COUPE

½ cup canned crushed pineapple
½ cup heavy cream
1 cup cottage cheese
¼ cup granulated sugar
¼ tsp. almond extract
1 pkg. (10 oz.) frozen sliced strawberries, thawed
2 tbsp. grenadine syrup

Drain crushed pineapple. Whip cream. Combine pineapple, cottage cheese, whipped cream, sugar, and almond extract in a bowl and refrigerate. Mix strawberries and grenadine syrup together. Refrigerate. To serve, alternate layers of cottage cheese mixture and strawberries in sherbet glasses. If desired, top each serving with a strawberry. Serves 6.

STRAWBERRIES IN WINE

1 pint fresh strawberries, hulled, cored, and cut in half
3 tbsp. sugar (optional)
½ cup white wine, champagne, or ginger ale

Sprinkle strawberries with sugar, if desired, and stir gently. Pour wine over berries. Cover and refrigerate at least one hour. Serves 4.

STRAWBERRIES, ALMONDS, AND WINE

1 cup grated blanched almonds
1½ cups sweet white wine
4 egg yolks
½ cup granulated sugar
Strawberries, hulled
Powdered sugar
Red currant jelly
Whipped cream tinted a delicate pink

Heat almonds and white wine over simmering water.

In a saucepan beat egg yolks and granulated sugar until sugar is dissolved. Gradually whisk in wine and almonds. Pour into a buttered and sugared 8-inch layer cake pan. Set pan in larger pan containing about an inch of hot water and bake in a preheated 325-degree oven for about 45 minutes, or until silver knife blade comes out clean. Cool and chill.

Unmold custard on chilled platter and arrange a pyramid of strawberries, which have been rolled in powdered sugar, in the center. Surround these strawberries with a crown of pink, whipped cream rosettes. Keep cold until serving time. Just before serving, surround with a ribbon of red currant jelly which has been heated and thinned with a little sweet wine or water to sauce consistency. Serves 4.

To serve: Add whole strawberries, hulled and rolled in confectioners' sugar.

STRAWBERRY CHARLOTTE DESSERT

2 pkgs. (10 oz.) frozen strawberries
2 envelopes unflavored gelatin
¾ cup sugar, divided
¼ tsp. salt
4 eggs, separated

½ cup water
2 tbsp. lemon juice
2 tsp. grated lemon rind
8 ladyfingers
1 cup heavy cream, whipped

Mix thoroughly the gelatin, ¼ cup of the sugar, and the salt in the top of a double boiler. Beat egg yolks and water together. Add to gelatin mixture. Add 1 package of the frozen sliced strawberries. Cook over boiling water, stirring constantly until gelatin is dissolved and strawberries thawed, about 8 minutes. Remove from heat and add remaining package of strawberries, lemon juice, and rind. Stir until berries are thawed. Chill in refrigerator or in bowl of ice and water, stirring occasionally, until the mixture mounds when dropped from spoon.

Split ladyfingers in half and stand around edge of an 8-inch springform pan. Beat egg whites until stiff. Beat in remaining ½ cup sugar. Fold in gelatin mixture. Fold in whipped cream. Turn into pan and chill until firm. Remove from pan and garnish with additional whipped cream and strawberries. Serves 10–12.

STRAWBERRY SOUFFLÉ

1 cup strawberries, slightly mashed and sweetened
  or 1 pkg. (10 oz.) frozen, sliced strawberries, thawed and drained
2 pkgs. (3 oz.) cream cheese, softened
½ cup sour cream
3 egg yolks
4 egg whites
1 tbsp. Cointreau, Grand Marnier, or Triple Sec

Mix cream cheese, sour cream, and egg yolks until smooth and creamy. Stir in berries and Cointreau. Beat egg whites until stiff and fold in gently. Put into a small buttered casserole with straight sides. Bake in 350-degree oven 50–60 minutes or until top springs back when lightly touched. For good timing, put this in the oven a few minutes before serving the main course.

MERINGUE GLACÉS

6 egg whites (room temperature)
⅛ tsp. salt
2 cups granulated sugar
1 tsp. vinegar
1 tsp. vanilla extract

Add salt to egg whites and beat until stiff enough to hold a shape. At low speed, add sugar, about 2 tablespoons at a time, beating 2 minutes after each addition. (This takes about half an hour.) Start heating oven to 275 degrees. Add vinegar and vanilla to the meringue and beat at high speed for another 10 minutes. Drop by heaping spoonfuls onto buttered cookie sheet. Bake for 45 minutes. Reduce heat to 250 degrees and bake another 15 minutes or until creamy white and firm. Remove to rack and cool. Cover the meringues lightly with waxed paper or foil; store in covered container until needed. To serve, meringues should be broken apart like a biscuit. The lower part may be filled with ice cream or whipped cream. Replace the top and spoon over strawberry or other favorite sauce.

BRANDIED STRAWBERRIES

3 pkgs. (10 oz. ea.) frozen sliced strawberries, thawed
1 tbsp. cornstarch
½ cup currant jelly
Red food color
¼ cup brandy

Drain berries slightly, saving ½ cup juice. Combine juice and cornstarch, stirring to dissolve lumps. Melt jelly over low heat and add cornstarch mixture. Cook, stirring over low heat until thickened and clear. Tint with food color. Add brandy and berries. Makes 2 cups. Goes well over vanilla or pistachio ice cream topped with meringue glacé.

DANISH DESSERT

Crust:
2 cups flour
½ cup brown sugar
1 cup butter
1 cup chopped nuts

Filling:
12 oz. cream cheese
2 pkgs. Dream Whip
1 cup powdered sugar
1 tsp. vanilla

Topping:
1 pkg. Danish strawberry dessert
1 pkg. (10 oz.) frozen strawberries

Blend crust ingredients and press into 9 × 13-inch pan. Bake 15 minutes at 350 degrees. Cool and crumble. Save half for topping and line bottom of pan with other half. Whip Dream Whip and add vanilla, powdered sugar, and cream cheese. Whip until creamy. Spread over crust. Sprinkle with remaining crumbs that were set aside for topping. Chill. Cook Danish dessert according to instructions on box. Add fruit. Spoon topping over cut pieces of dessert as served.

HONEY-SAUTERNE STRAWBERRIES

Mix ¼ cup honey and ¼ cup sauterne or other sweet white wine. Divide ½ cup strawberries among 4 dessert dishes and spoon 2 tablespoons honey mixture onto each serving.

STRAWBERRY-RHUBARB PUFF

1 pkg. (16 oz.) frozen rhubard, thawed
1 pkg. (10 oz.) frozen strawberries, thawed
½ cup sugar
2 cups flour
2 tbsp. sugar
3 tsp. baking powder
1 tsp. salt
½ cup salad oil
⅔ cup milk
Butter or margarine
2 tbsp. sugar
1 tsp. cinnamon

Heat oven to 450 degrees. Mix rhubarb, strawberries (with syrup), and ½ cup sugar in ungreased 9 × 9 × 2-inch square pan. Heat this mixture in oven while preparing the biscuit topping.

Measure flour, 2 tablespoons sugar, baking powder, and salt in bowl. Pour oil and milk into measuring cup, pouring all at once into flour mixture, then stir until mixture cleans side of bowl and forms a ball. Dot with butter. Mix 2 tablespoons sugar and the cinnamon and sprinkle over dough. Bake 20–25 minutes or until topping is golden brown. Serve warm with light cream or whipped cream if desired. Serves 9.

STRAWBERRIES JUBILEE

1 pint strawberries, hulled and cored
½ cup water
⅓ cup sugar
2 tsp. arrowroot or cornstarch
2 ounces kirsch
1 quart vanilla ice cream

Mix water, sugar, and arrowroot (or cornstarch). Bring to a boil, stirring, and add strawberries. Return to a boil, stirring only enough to blend. Add kirsch and ignite. Serve the flaming sauce and strawberries over the ice cream. Serves 6.

STRAWBERRY TAPIOCA

Mix in saucepan:
2½ cups strawberry juice (sweetened berries crushed, with water added)
½ cup sugar
¼ cup quick-cooking tapioca
¼ tsp. salt

Cook over low heat, stirring constantly, until mixture boils. Remove from heat. Cool.

Fold in:
1 cup sliced strawberries
1 tbsp. lemon juice

Spoon into dessert dishes. Serves 6.

STRAWBERRIES AND SOUR CREAM

2 pints strawberries, hulled, cored, and sliced
⅔ cup sour cream
⅓ cup light brown sugar
Brown sugar (for topping)
Sour cream (for topping)

In a bowl combine strawberries, sour cream, and brown sugar. Place in individual serving dishes and top each with 1 tablespoon sour cream and 1 teaspoon brown sugar.

FLAMBÉD STRAWBERRY OMELET

2 cups crushed strawberries
¼ cup sugar or 2 tbsp. honey
¼ cup sherry
2 tbsp. kirsch or other liqueur
4 eggs, separated
½ tsp. salt
Pinch of pepper and salt
½ cup heavy cream
1 tbsp. unsalted butter
Superfine sugar
¼ cup light rum, warmed

Combine berries, the ¼ cup sugar or honey, sherry, and kirsch and let stand one hour. When ready to make the omelet, preheat oven to 350 degrees. Beat egg yolks, adding salt, pepper, and cream.

Beat egg whites until stif but not dry. Fold into egg yolk mixture. Melt butter in a 9-inch ovenproof skillet. When hot, pour in egg mixture and cook over low heat 3–5 minutes or until omelet puffs and is browned on the bottom. Place in oven for 10–15 minutes, until top springs back when touched with finger. Slip omelet onto a hot platter when ready to serve. Meanwhile, in a saucepan, heat berry mixture but do not boil. Pour over and around omelet and sprinkle with superfine sugar. Pour rum over berries. Ignite, standing back cautiously, and serve flaming. Serves 6.

BAKED ALASKA SUPREME

One sponge cake baked in a round 10-inch pan, **half of your favorite recipe**
½ tsp. cream of tartar
6 egg whites
1 cup sugar
2 quarts strawberry ice cream, softened

Place cake on a bread board. Whip egg whites and cream of tartar until stiff. Gradually beat in sugar 1 tablespoon at a time and continue beating until meringue is stiff and glossy. Pile ice cream on top of cake. Refreeze until very hard. Completely cover ice cream and sides of cake with meringue. Place in 500-degree oven for 3-5 minutes or until lightly browned. Slip dessert on serving platter and serve at once.

JELLY ROLL

3 eggs
1 cup granulated sugar
⅓ cup water
1 tsp. vanilla
¾ cup all-purpose flour* or 1 cup cake flour
1 tsp. baking powder
¼ tsp. salt
About ⅔ cup jelly or jam
Powdered sugar
*Omit baking powder and salt if using self-rising flour.

Heat oven to 375 degrees. Line a 15 × 10 × ½-inch jelly roll pan with aluminum foil or waxed paper; grease generously. Beat eggs in small mixing bowl on high speed until thick and lemon-colored, about 5 minutes. Pour eggs into large mixing bowl. Beat in sugar gradually. Add water and vanilla, beating at slow speed. Add flour, baking powder, and salt gradually, beating only until batter is smooth. Pour into pan. Bake until wooden pick inserted in center comes out clean, 12–15 minutes. Loosen cake from edges of pan immediately, and invert on towel sprinkled with powdered sugar. Carefully remove foil. Trim off stiff edges if necessary.

While it is hot, starting from short side roll up cake and towel. Cool on wire rack 30 minutes. Unroll cake and remove towel. Whip jelly slightly with fork to soften; spread over cake. Reroll and sprinkle with powdered sugar. Serves 10.

Rainbow Sherbet Roll: Omit jelly. Instead spread raspberry sherbet on ⅓ of cake, orange sherbet on next ⅓, and lime sherbet on remaining cake. Roll up but do not sprinkle with powdered sugar. Place seam side down on piece of aluminum foil, 28 × 12 inches. Wrap securely in foil and freeze. Remove from freezer 15 minutes before serving. Serves 12.

Strawberry Roll: Omit jelly. About 1 hour before serving, beat ½ cup chilled whipped cream and 2 tablespoons powdered sugar until stiff. Spread on unrolled cake. Arrange 2 cups sliced fresh strawberries on top of whipped cream. Roll up. Sprinkle with powdered sugar and refrigerate. Serve with sweetened whipped cream. Serves 8–10.

Sweetened Whipped Cream: Beat until stiff ½ cup whipping cream and 1 tablespoon granulated or powdered sugar in a chilled bowl. Makes one cup.

CHOCOLATE-PAINTED STRAWBERRY FANS

This dessert is not only chic, it's also light tasting, low-cal, and easy!

12 extra-large strawberries with stems
3 sq. (3 oz. ea.) semisweet chocolate or chocolate-flavored candy coating
3 oz. white baking pieces with cocoa butter or vanilla-flavored candy coating
Powdered sugar
Unsweetened cocoa powder

Rinse strawberries and pat dry. Leave caps and stems intact. With a sharp knife, make four or five slices in each berry from the tip and almost to, but not through, the cap. Gently fan out berry as far as possible (stem end of berry should remain intact).

Separately chop semisweet chocolate and white baking pieces or candy coatings. Melt each in a separate heavy saucepan over low heat, stirring constantly. Remove from heat. On each of four dessert plates, cover a portion of the plate with a sheet of paper. Lightly sift powdered sugar over the exposed portion of the plate. Lift paper and lie it down to cover the powdered sugar on the plate. Lightly sift cocoa powder over the exposed portion of the plate and carefully lift off paper. Arrange three or four strawberry fans atop each plate. Using a small spoon, drizzle melted chocolate over berries and plate, then drizzle the melted white baking pieces over a portion of the berries. Serve immediately. Makes 4 servings.

MOLDED STRAWBERRY CRÈME

2 pkgs. (3 oz. each) strawberry gelatin
½ cup sugar
¼ tsp. salt
2 cups boiling water
½ cup cold water
½ cup mashed strawberries
1 cup heavy cream

Combine gelatin, sugar, and salt in a bowl. Add boiling water and stir until gelatin is dissolved. Stir in the cold water and juice from strawberries. Cool. Chill until mixture is slightly thickened. Add the cream and beat with a rotary beater until just blended. Fold in strawberries. Turn into a 5-cup mold. Chill until firm, about 4 hours. Unmold and invert on a chilled plate.

STRAWBERRY ANGEL LOAF

1 angel food cake loaf
1 quart strawberry ice cream
2 cups cream, whipped
1 cup miniature marshmallows
½ cup chopped walnuts
⅔ cup crushed pineapple, well drained
2 cups fresh strawberries, sliced and sweetened to taste

Slice the cake in half lengthwise. Spread ice cream between the two halves, sandwich style. Combine all remaining ingredients and frost the loaf. Store in freezer until ready to serve.

STRAWBERRIES AND ALMONDS

1 quart fresh strawberries, hulled and cored
¼ cup raspberry jam
2 tbsp. sugar
¼ cup water
1 tbsp. kirsch
¼ cup slivered blanched almonds

Combine jam, sugar, and water in a saucepan and simmer about 2 minutes. Add kirsch and chill. Arrange strawberries in 4 individual serving dishes. Pour chilled raspberry sauce over the fruit and sprinkle with the slivered almonds. Serves 4.

5. PIES, TORTES, JAMS AND JELLIES, CANDIES

I made a pie and it was good;
It came out just as good pies should.
I made some coffee, fragrant, strong,
But sadly, no one came along.
I made a pie and it was punk:
It swelled — and then it went "kerplunk."
I made some coffee, "twas weak and thin,"
And all that day my friends dropped in.

STRAWBERRY PIE I

½ cup or more chopped pecans
2 unbaked pastry crusts (9-inch)
1 pkg. (8 oz.) cream cheese
1 cup sugar
1 tsp. vanilla
1 pint whipping cream, whipped
Fresh or frozen strawberries

Press pecan pieces into pie shells and bake according to pastry recipe, taking care not to burn the pecans. Cream together cream cheese, sugar, and vanilla until fluffy. Mix the whipped cream into the mixture and pour into shells. Top with thawed, drained whole strawberries and chill. Makes 2 pies.

STRAWBERRY PIE II

1 pkg. D-Zerta gelatin
1 cup boiling water
1 box (20 oz.) frozen strawberries, broken into chunks
1 graham cracker pie shell
1 cup whipped topping

Dissolve D-Zerta gelatin in boiling water, then add frozen strawberries. Stir until strawberries are separated and spoon into prepared crust. Refrigerate until firm. Top with swirls of whipped topping. Serves 5 or 6.

FRESH STRAWBERRY PIE

1 baked and cooled pie shell
1 envelope strawberry D-Zerta
1 quart strawberries, washed, hulled, and cored
Whipped topping

Prepare D-Zerta according to package instructions and chill until slightly thickened. Put strawberries in pie shell and spoon the thickened D-Zerta over berries. Chill until set. Spoon topping around the inside edge of the pie crust.

STRAWBERRY MINUTE PIE

1 pkg. (3 oz.) strawberry gelatin
1 cup boiling water
1 pkg. frozen, sweetened, sliced strawberries
1 baked pie shell (8-inch)

Dissolve gelatin in water. Add unthawed berries, breaking them up with a fork. As berries thaw, gelatin will thicken. When partially set, pour into cooled pie shell. Chill until completely set. Serve with whipped cream. Serves 6.

WHIPPED STRAWBERRY PIE

1 box strawberry Whip 'n Chill
1 box (10 oz.) frozen strawberries
1 graham cracker pie shell (9-inch)
Whipped topping

Prepare Whip 'n Chill according to package directions, using juice from thawed strawberries for part of the water. Add drained strawberries, reserving 6 for garnish. Pour into prepared pie shell. Chill for at least 2 hours. Serve each piece of pie with a spoonful of whipped topping and one of the reserved strawberries. Serves 6.

STRAWBERRY ICE BOX PIE

1 pkg. (17 oz.) marshmallows
1 box (16 oz.) frozen strawberries or 2 cups sweetened fresh strawberries
1 cup whipping cream, whipped
1 baked pastry shell (9-inch), chilled

Put marshmallows in a double boiler; add 2 tablespoons strawberry juice. Cook until marshmallows are melted. Add strawberries and mix thoroughly. Chill about 2 hours. Fold in whipped cream and pour mixture into the cold baked pastry shell. Serves 8.

LADY BIRD'S STRAWBERRY ICE BOX PIE

1 17-ounce pkg. marshmallows
1 box (16 oz.) frozen strawberries or 2 cups fresh strawberries, hulled, cored,
 and sweetened to taste
1 cup whipping cream, whipped
1 cooled pastry shell

Put marshmallows in double boiler. Add two tablespoons of strawberry juice (or water if using fresh berries). Cook until marshmallows are dissolved. Mix strawberries and marshmallows thoroughly. Chill about two hours. Fold whipped cream in marshmallow mixture and pour into pastry shell. Chill until firm.

STRAWBERRY ICE CREAM PIE

1¼ cups boiling water
1 pkg. (3 oz.) strawberry gelatin
1 pint strawberry ice cream
1 cup strawberries

Dissolve gelatin in boiling water and stir in 1 pint of strawberry ice cream. Let set until it starts to congeal. Fold in 1 cup fresh or frozen strawberries.

FROZEN STRAWBERRY PIE I

1 large can evaporated milk, chilled
1 pkg. (3 oz.) strawberry gelatin
1 cup sugar
1 pkg. (10 oz.) frozen strawberries
2 graham cracker pie crusts (8-inch)

Whip milk with electric mixer at high speed until very stiff. Reduce speed and add gelatin and sugar. Fold in strawberries and pour into pie shells. Freeze until firm. Serves 12.

FROZEN STRAWBERRY PIE II

1 8-oz. package cream cheese, softened
1 cup dairy sour cream
2 10-oz. pkgs. frozen sliced strawberries, thawed
1 9-inch graham cracker crust

Blend cream cheese and sour cream. Reserve ½ cup berries and syrup. Add remaining berries and syrup to cheese mixture and pour into crust. Freeze firm. Remove from freezer 5 minutes before serving. Cut into wedges and serve topped with reserved strawberries in syrup.

FROZEN STRAWBERRY-YOGURT PIE

2 cartons (8 oz.) vanilla yogurt
3½ cups whipped topping, thawed
2 cups sliced or finely chopped strawberries, sweetened
1 graham cracker crumb crust

Fold yogurt into whipped topping. Blend well and fold in strawberries. Spoon into crust. Freeze until firm, four hours or overnight. Garnish with additional whole strawberries if desired. Let stand at room temperature 10 minutes before serving. Note: Store leftover pie in freezer.

STRAWBERRY PARFAIT PIE

1 3-oz. package strawberry-flavored gelatin
1 pint vanilla ice cream
1 cup sliced fresh strawberries
1 9-inch baked pastry shell, cooled

Dissolve gelatin in 1¼ cups boiling water. Add the ice cream by spoonfuls, stirring until melted. Chill until the mixture mounds slightly when dropped from a spoon. Gently fold in sliced strawberries. Turn into pastry shell and chill until firm. If desired, serve topped with whipped cream and extra strawberries.

STRAWBERRY GELATIN-BAVARIAN PIE

1 3-oz. pkg. strawberry gelatin
1 tbsp. sugar
⅛ tsp. salt
1 cup boiling water
½ cup cold water
1 10-oz. pkg. frozen strawberries
1 cup whipped topping, thawed
1 baked 9-inch pie shell, cooled

Dissolve gelatin, sugar, and salt in boiling water. Add the cold water and frozen strawberries. Stir gently until fruit thaws and separates. Chill until slightly thickened. Add whipped topping and blend until smooth. (Mixture may appear slightly curdled but will smooth out on blending.) Pour into pie shell. Chill until firm, about 4 hours. Garnish with additional whipped topping, fresh whole strawberries, and mint leaves if desired.

STRAWBERRY CREAM PIE I

1 pkg. (10 oz.) frozen strawberries
1 pkg. (3 oz.) strawberry gelatin
1 pint vanilla ice cream
1 9-inch graham cracker crust, cooled

Heat strawberries to boiling, breaking apart with fork. Stir in gelatin until dissolved. Mix in ice cream until melted. Chill until thickened but not set. Pour into prepared crust. Chill until firm, about 2 hours. Serve with whipped cream or dessert topping.

STRAWBERRY CREAM PIE II

For crust:
20 graham crackers, rolled into crumbs
½ stick butter or margarine, softened
½ cup sugar

Mix all together and pat into 9 × 13-inch cake pan.

For filling, cream with electric mixer:
12 oz. cream cheese
2 eggs
¾ cup sugar
1 tsp. vanilla

Pour filling over the graham cracker crust. Bake in 350 degree oven and cool. Drain two packages (10 oz.) frozen strawberries. Thicken the berry juice with cornstarch, adding enough sugar to taste. Spread over the baked cooled pie and chill.

STRAWBERRY SOUR CREAM PIE I

1 crumb crust (9-inch)
1½ cups sliced strawberries
1 cup sugar
1 egg white
1 cup sour cream

Combine strawberries, sugar, and egg white. Whip until creamy with electric mixer. Fold in sour cream. Freeze. Granish with strawberries before serving.

100

STRAWBERRY SOUR CREAM PIE II

1 cup dairy sour cream
1 cup milk
1 pkg. (4 oz.) chocolate instant pudding and pie filling
1½ cups sliced strawberries

Beat sour cream and milk with a hand beater until smooth. Mix in dry pudding and pie filling until smooth and slightly thickened. Pour into graham cracker crust (below). Arrange strawberries over the filling and pour strawberry glacé over strawberries. Refrigerate until firm (2 hours) and top with whipped cream if desired.

Graham Cracker Crust:

Mix 1½ cups graham cracker crumbs with 3 tablespoons sugar and ⅓ cup melted butter or margarine. Press mixture firmly and evenly in 9-inch ungreased pie plate. Bake 10 minutes at 350 degrees.

STRAWBERRY-CHEESE PIE
(No calorie watchers here — a little goes a long way!)

1 graham cracker crust, baked 10 minutes
2 eggs
1 pkg. (16 oz.) cream cheese
½ pint and 3 tbsp. sour cream
Dash salt
¾ cup and 2 tbsp. sugar
2 tsp. vanilla
Lemon juice

Beat eggs with a mixer and blend in cheese, 3 tablespoons sour cream, dash of salt, ¾ cup sugar, and 1 teaspoon vanilla. Bake for 20 minutes in 375-degree oven. Remove from oven and pour over ½ pint sour cream which has been mixed with 2 tablespoons sugar, one teaspoon vanilla and sprinkle of lemon juice. Bake at 425 degrees for 5 minutes. Cool. Refrigerate overnight.

Bring to boil:

1 pkg. (16 oz.) frozen strawberries
¼ cup water mixed with
½ tbsp. cornstarch

Cool. Save some of the mixture for glazing strawberries and pour the rest over pie. Place whole strawberries on pie and pour on glaze.

101

FLUFFY BERRY CHEESE PIE

1 baked and cooled 9-inch pie shell
1 cup miniature marshmallows
½ cup milk
1 pkg. (3 oz.) strawberry gelatin
½ cup water
1 pkg. (3 oz.) cream cheese, softened
1 pkg. (10 oz.) frozen strawberries, thawed
½ cup whipping cream

Heat miniature marshmallows and milk in saucepan over medium-low heat, stirring until marshmallows are melted. Set aside. In a saucepan, mix strawberry gelatin and water. Heat and stir until dissolved. Combine marshmallow mixture with gelatin and gradually beat in the softened cream cheese. Drain thawed strawberries, reserving syrup. Add water to syrup to equal ¼ cup liquid. Stir strawberry syrup into the gelatin mixture and chill until the mixture is partially set. Whip the mixture and fold in strawberries. Whip the cream and fold in. Chill again until the mixture mounds when spooned, and then pile the strawberry mixture into the pie shell. Chill 3 to 4 hours or until the filling is set. Make the pie festive with dollops of whipped cream and strawberries.

STRAWBERRY GLACÉ PIE

1 9-inch pie shell
6 cups fresh strawberries, hulled and cored
1 cup sugar
3 tbsp. cornstarch
½ cup water
1 pkg. (3 oz.) cream cheese, softened

Prepare and bake 9-inch pie shell. Mash enough berries to measure 1 cup. Stir together sugar and cornstarch. Gradually stir in water and crushed strawberries. Cook over medium heat, stirring constantly, until mixture thickens and boils. Boil and stir 1 minute. Cool. Beat cream cheese until smooth and spread on bottom of baked pie shell. Fill the shell with remaining berries. Pour the cooked berry mixture on top. Chill 3 hours or until set.

STRAWBERRY-RHUBARB PIE I

Pastry for two-crust pie
1 pint fresh strawberries, washed, hulled, and cored
2 cups sliced raw rhubarb
¾ cup brown sugar
½ cup granulated sugar
1 tsp. grated lemon rind

Slice strawberries and rhubarb. Combine the sugars and lemon rind and toss lightly with fruit. Pour into pie shell. Cover with top crust, sealing edges. Bake at 350 degrees for 50 minutes.

STRAWBERRY-RHUBARB PIE II

Pastry for two-crust pie with lattice top
1¼ cups sugar
⅓ cup all-purpose flour
Pinch salt
1 tsp. orange zest
1 pound fresh rhubarb, cut in 1-inch pieces
2 cups strawberries, washed, hulled, and cored
2 tbsp. butter or margarine
1 tsp. milk
1 tbsp. sugar

Preheat the oven to 425 degrees. In a large bowl, combine sugar, flour, salt, and orange zest. Add strawberries and rhubarb and toss lightly to mix. Set aside.

In rolling out the bottom portion of the pie dough allow for a 1-inch overhang. Spoon filling in and dot with butter. For lattice top roll the dough out in a rectangle and cut ten ½-inch wide strips. Weave the lattice top and trim ends. Moisten the overhanging edge of the bottom crust and fold up over the strip ends. Flute edge of crust. Brush lattice strips with milk and sprinkle with the tablespoon of sugar. Place the pie on a baking sheet and bake in lower part of oven for 15 minutes. Reduce heat to 350 degrees and bake 50 minutes more until bubbly and golden brown. Cool the pie on a wire rack and serve warm at room temperature with whipped topping or vanilla yogurt.

FRENCH STRAWBERRY GLACÉ PIE

1 8-inch or 9-inch baked pie shell
1 quart strawberries
1 cup water
1 cup sugar
3 tbsp. cornstarch
1 pkg. (3 oz.) cream cheese

Wash, drain, and hull strawberries. Simmer ⅔ cup water and one cup strawberries for 3 minutes. Blend in sugar, cornstarch, and ⅓ cup water. Boil one minute, stirring constantly. Cool. Spread softened cream cheese over bottom of cooled pie shell. Save ½ cup of the choice berries. Put remaining 2½ cups of berries in pie shell. Cover with cooked mixture. Garnish with the ½ cup berries. Refrigerate about 2 hours or until firm. Serve with whipped cream or ice cream.

DEEP-DISH RHUBARB-STRAWBERRY PIE

¾ cup sugar
⅓ cup sifted all-purpose flour
1 tsp. cinnamon
1 tsp. cloves
1 pound fresh rhubarb cut in 1-inch pieces
1 pint strawberries, hulled, cored, and cut in half
2 tbsp. butter or margarine

Mix sugar, flour, cinnamon, and cloves together. Combine strawberries with rhubarb in a large bowl and sprinkle with the sugar mixture, stirring lightly to mix. Let stand 15 minutes and again mix lightly. Spoon rhubarb-strawberry filling into an 8 × 8 × 2-inch baking dish. Dot with butter or margarine.

Prepare pastry and roll out to a 10-inch square on a lightly floured surface. Cut in ½-inch strips and weave strips into a lattice to cover filling. Turn ends under just enough so that strips touch sides of baking dish. Brush lattice top with milk or cream and sprinkle with sugar. Bake in a 425-degree oven for 40 minutes or until pastry is golden and juices bubble up. Cool and serve warm with vanilla ice cream if desired.

FROZEN STRAWBERRY-CHEESE PIE

1 baked and cooled 9-inch pie shell
1 pkg. (8 oz.) cream cheese, softened
1 cup dairy sour cream
2 pkgs. (10 oz. each) frozen sliced strawberries, thawed

Blend cream cheese and sour cream. Reserve ½ cup berries and syrup. Mix remaining berries and syrup into cheese mixture. Pour filling into baked pie shell. Cover and freeze until firm. To serve, let the pie thaw enough to cut, about 15–30 minutes. Serve topped with reserved berries in syrup.

STRAWBERRY CHIFFON PIE I

1 9-inch baked pastry shell with fluted edges
1 pint (1½ cups) fresh strawberries, hulled and cored
¾ cup sugar
1 tbsp. lemon juice
1 envelope unflavored gelatin
¾ cup water
2 egg whites
½ cup whipping cream

Reserve five or six strawberries and chill for garnish. Crush strawberries and stir in ¼ cup of the sugar and the lemon juice. Let stand 30 minutes. In a small saucepan stir another ¼ cup sugar and gelatin. Add the water. Heat and stir until sugar and gelatin dissolve. Cool. Stir the cooled gelatin mixture into the strawberry mixture and chill until partially set, stirring occasionally.

In a mixing bowl beat egg whites until soft peaks form and gradually add the remaining ¼ cup sugar, beating until stiff peaks form. Fold the egg white mixture into the strawberry mixture. Beat whipping cream until soft peaks form and fold into the strawberry mixture. Chill if necessary until the mixture mounds. Pour into cooled pastry shell. Chill at least 8 hours until filling is firm. Garnish with the reserved strawberries (either whole or halved) and additional whipped cream if desired.

STRAWBERRY CHIFFON PIE II

1 9-inch baked pie shell
4 cups (2 pints) strawberries
1 cup sugar
2 envelopes unflavored gelatin
½ cup water
3 egg whites
1½ cups heavy cream

Wash strawberries, hull, and core. Slice enough to make 3 cups, reserving the remainder for garnish. Combine sliced strawberries and ½ cup of the sugar in a bowl. Let stand 5 minutes, then mash well or press through a sieve into a large bowl. Soften the gelatin in water in a small saucepan. Heat slowly until gelatin dissolves. Cool slightly, then stir into strawberry mixture. Place bowl in a pan of water with ice to speed setting. Chill, stirring several times until mixture begins to thicken.

Meanwhile, beat egg whites in a bowl until foamy white. Slowly beat in remaining ½ cup sugar until the meringue stands in firm peaks. Beat 1 cup of the cream until stiff. Fold meringue, then whipped cream into strawberry mixture until the color appears even throughout. Pour into cooled pastry shell. Chill until firm. Before serving, beat the remaining cream until stiff and spoon it on the center of the pie. Garnish with the remaining strawberries.

Strawberry Glacé:
½ cup sliced strawberries
½ cup water
½ cup sugar
1 tbsp. plus 1½ tsp. cornstarch

Heat strawberries and ¼ cup of the water to simmering in 1-quart saucepan. Simmer uncovered for 3 minutes. Mix sugar and cornstarch in small bowl and stir in remaining ¼ cup water. Stir into hot strawberry mixture. Cook, stirring constantly, until mixture thickens and boils. Boil and stir 1 minute.

BERRY BASKET PIE

4 cups fresh strawberries, hulled and cored
1 envelope (2 oz.) dessert topping mix
1 can (18 oz.) vanilla pudding

Prepare your favorite 9-inch vanilla wafer or cookie crumb crust. Arrange the whole prepared berries in the crust, reserving 8 berries for garnish. Prepare dessert topping according to directions on package and add to the can of prepared pudding. Pour mixture onto berries in crust. Chill 4 hours and garnish with berries.

DEEP DISH STRAWBERRY AND APPLE PIE

Crust:

½ cup all-purpose flour
½ cup whole wheat flour
½ tsp. salt
½ cup solid vegetable shortening, chilled
3 tbsp. ice water
1 tbsp. fresh lemon juice

Mix flour and salt and cut shortening in with pastry blender or knives until mixture resembles coarse meal. Add water and lemon juice, mixing with fork. Divide dough in two and roll out one portion to line an 8 × 8-inch baking pan or a 10-inch deep dish pie pan. Roll out other half of dough to cover.

Filling:

1½ cups sugar
1½ tbsp. cornstarch
1 tsp. cinnamon
4 large tart apples, peeled, cored, and thinly sliced
1 pint strawberries, cored and halved
1 tbsp. butter

Preheat oven to 400 degrees. Combine sugar, cornstarch, and cinnamon in a 3-quart mixing bowl. Add apples and toss to coat evenly. Arrange half in lined pan. Layer with half the strawberries. Repeat with remaining apple slices and then remaining strawberries. Dot with butter. Cover with top crust and cut vents. Bake until crust is firm and lightly browned, about 30 minutes.

STRAWBERRY MERINGUE PIE
(Luscious! The meringue is the crust.)

3 egg whites
½ tsp. baking powder
1 cup sugar
10 soda crackers (2 inches sq.), rolled fine
½ cup cut-up pecans
1 pint strawberries
½ cup whipped cream, sweetened to taste

Beat egg whites with ½ teaspoon baking powder until stiff, gradually beating in the cup of sugar. Fold in the cracker crumbs and pecans. Spread in a well-buttered 9-inch pie pan. Bake in a 300-degree (slow) oven for 30 minutes. Cool. Fill with the pint of unsweetened strawberries and top with sweetened whipped cream.

MERINGUE SHELL

3 egg whites
1 tsp. vanilla
¼ tsp. cream of tartar
Dash salt
1 cup sugar

Have egg whites at room temperature. Add vanilla, cream of tartar and salt. Beat until soft peaks form. Gradually add sugar, beating until very stiff peaks form and sugar is dissolved. (Meringue will be glossy.) Cover a baking sheet with plain, ungreased brown paper. Using a 9-inch round cake pan as a guide, draw a circle on paper and spread the meringue over the circle. Shape into a shell with the back of large spoon, making the bottom ½-inch thick and the sides about 1¾ inches high. Bake at 275 degrees for one hour. Turn off the heat and let the shell dry with oven door closed for at least 2 hours. Makes one 9-inch meringue shell.

STRAWBERRY SATIN PIE

1 baked 9-inch pastry shell
½ cup sliced almonds, toasted

To assemble pie, cover bottom of cooled pastry shell with almonds. Fill with chilled creamy satin filling.

Creamy satin filling:
½ cup sugar
3 tbsp. cornstarch
3 tbsp. all-purpose flour
½ tsp. salt
2 cups milk
1 slightly beaten egg
½ cup whipping cream
1 tsp. vanilla

Combine sugar, cornstarch, and flour and gradually stir in milk. Bring to a boil, stirring constantly. Lower the heat, cooking and stirring until creamy and bubbly. Stir a little of the hot mixture in the beaten egg and return this to the remaining hot mixture. Bring just to a boil, stirring constantly, then chill thoroughly. Beat well. Whip the cream and fold into egg mixture with vanilla.

Berry mixture:
3 cups fresh strawberries
¼ cup sugar
2 tsp. cornstarch
Few drops red food coloring
Whipped cream

Divide strawberries as follows: Reserve a few perfect berries for center. Crush ½ cup berries and set aside; halve remaining berries. Arrange halved and whole berries atop filling.

Combine ½ cup crushed berries and ½ cup water. Cook 2 minutes, then sieve. Mix sugar and cornstarch, and gradually stir in berry juice. Cook and stir until thick and clear. Tint with red food coloring. Cool mixture slightly and spoon over pie. Refrigerate until serving time. Top with whipped cream.

ANGEL PIE

Using a meringue shell, a dainty dessert can be made with a cream filling and a whipped cream topping with fruit garnish. Angel pie is usually made in an 8- or 9-inch size. Cream fillings such as lemon, orange, and strawberry are commonly used. Fold fruit into filling or just use sweetened fresh fruit in the meringue shell. Ice cream balls may be piled into the shell and topped with chocolate, butterscotch, or fruit sauce. The shell and filling can be made the night before or several hours in advance of serving time, thus eliminating last-minute preparation. Show off this attractive dessert and save time, too, by slicing and serving it at the table.

MILE-HIGH STRAWBERRY PIE

1 prebaked 10-inch pie shell with edges fluted high
4 pints ripe strawberries with fresh green stems
1 pint heavy cream, whipped
1⅓ ounces tapioca flour (not granulated tapioca)
2 tsp. unflavored gelatin, softened in 2 tbsp. cold water

Wash berries in large sieve; shake and place on paper towels to dry. Reserve 8 large, perfect berries with stems for garnish. Remove stems from remainder of berries, setting side less-than-perfect berries to crush for making the glaze. Of remaining berries, leave larger ones whole but cut smaller ones in half.

Glaze:

1½ cups sugar
½ cup white corn syrup
1½ cups crushed strawberries
1 tsp. fresh lemon juice, strained

Boil sugar, corn syrup and crushed berries together for 5 minutes in a saucepan, stirring constantly. Add lemon juice. Beat in tapioca flour a little at a time and cook, stirring, until thickened. Add softened gelatin. Remove from heat, strain, and let mixture cool partially. Brush about 2 tablespoons glaze over bottom and sides of pastry shell. Place large berries stem ends down in bottom of pastry shell and arrange in mound in center, filling in the spaces between with halved berries. Build berries high into a pyramid. When all berries are placed, spoon most of the warm glaze over all the berries and let the pie set in refrigerator for 1 hour before serving.

To serve, dip the 8 reserved berries with stems in the remaining glaze and set the berries around the top with stems up. Using a pastry bag, decorate the pie by building a huge collar around the edge with the whipped cream. Serves 8.

STRAWBERRY-CHOCOLATE COMBO

1 pkg. (6 oz.) instant chocolate pudding mix
1 loaf (10¾ oz.) frozen pound cake, thawed
1 can (21 oz.) strawberry pie filling, chilled
1 carton (8 oz.) frozen whipped topping, thawed

Prepare pudding mix according to package directions and set aside. Cut cake into ¾-inch cubes. Place in a 12 × 8 × 2-inch baking dish. Spread pudding over cake. Spoon pie filling over pudding. Top with whipped topping. Chill 2-3 hours. Yields 12-15 servings.

STRAWBERRY BLACK BOTTOM PIE

1 baked pie shell
⅔ cup half-and-half cream
1 pkg. (6 oz.) semisweet chocolate morsels
3 eggs, separated
2 pints fresh strawberries, hulled and cored
2 tsp. lemon juice
¼ cup sugar
1 pkg. unflavored gelatin
¼ cup cold water

Heat the half-and-half in a saucepan over medium heat. Stir in the chocolate morsels and beat smooth with wire whisk. Remove from heat. Whisk in the egg yolks one at a time, mixing until well blended. Return to heat. Cook, stirring, 1 or 2 minutes longer. Cool and pour into pie shell. Chill until set (2-3 hours).

Puree one pint of the strawberries with the lemon juice (will equal about 1⅔ cups puree). Soften gelatin in water; warm over low heat to dissolve, then stir in the berry puree. Chill until the mixture begins to set. Meanwhile, beat the egg whites while gradually adding the sugar until soft peaks form. Fold in the thickened berry mixture and pour this over the chocolate layer. Chill until set. To serve, slice the remaining pint of strawberries. Sweeten if desired and spoon over wedges of pie. Serves 6-8.

STRAWBERRY ANGEL PIE I

3 eggs, separated
¼ tsp. cream of tartar
¾ cup sugar
1 pkg. lemon pie filling
1 cup sliced strawberries
½ pint whipped cream
Whole strawberries

Beat egg whites until frothy. Add cream of tartar and beat until stiff. Add sugar slowly, beating until thick and glossy. Line pie pan and sides with meringue, bringing it up to form a ruffly edge. Bake at 275 degrees for one hour. Cool. While cooling, prepare pie filling as directed on package, using 3 egg yolks. While the meringue is still hot, stir in the sliced strawberries. Cool and spoon into pie shell. Chill. Top with whipped cream and whole berries.

STRAWBERRY ANGEL PIE II

1 pkg. (3 oz.) strawberry-flavored gelatin
1 cup sliced fresh strawberries or one 10 oz. package frozen sliced
    strawberries, thawed and drained
1 cup whipping cream
1 recipe meringue shell

Dissolve gelatin in 1¼ cups boiling water. Chill until gelatin mixture is partially set. Whip cream until soft peaks form. Fold cream and strawberries into the gelatin mixture. Chill until the mixture mounds slightly when spooned, then pile it into the meringue shell. Chill 4–5 hours or overnight. Top with additional whipped cream and berries if desired. Serves 8.

(In order to save time, the angel pie filling can be made from a pudding and pie filling mix, with canned or frozen fruit. Top with whipped topping and fruit garnish.)

HEAVENLY CHOCOLATE-BERRY PIE

1¼ cups graham cracker crumbs
3 tbsp. sugar
⅓ cup butter or margarine, melted
½ cup plus 2 tbsp. semisweet chocolate morsels, divided
1 pkg. (8 oz.) cream cheese, softened
¼ cup firmly packed brown sugar
½ tsp. vanilla extract
1 cup whipping cream, whipped
1 pint fresh strawberries
1 tsp. shortening

Combine the first 3 ingredients, mixing well. Firmly press into the bottom and sides of a lightly greased 9-inch pie plate. Bake at 325 degrees for 10 minutes. Cool the crust completely. Place ½ cup chocolate morsels in the top of a double boiler and bring water to a boil. Reduce heat to low and cook until chocolate melts. Set chocolate aside to cool slightly. Beat the cream cheese with an electric mixer until light and fluffy. Add brown sugar and vanilla, mixing well. Add the cooled chocolate, mixing well. Fold the whipped cream into the cream cheese mixture and spoon the filling into the prepared crust. Chill at least 8 hours.

Set aside one strawberry and cut the remaining strawberries into thick slices. Arrange the slices over the filling. Place a whole strawberry in the center. Combine the remaining 2 tablespoons of chocolate morsels and the shortening in a small saucepan over low heat. Cook until the chocolate melts. Drizzle over strawberries. Yields one 9-inch pie.

CALIFORNIA STRAWBERRY PIE

Prebaked 9-inch pie shell or your favorite crumb crust
1 quart hulled and cored strawberries
3 tbsp. cornstarch
½ cup water
1 cup granulated sugar
2 tbsp. lemon juice
½ cup heavy cream, whipped

Select about half of the smaller strawberries and mash these with the sugar, cornstarch, and water. Cook over medium heat, stirring until clear and thickened. Add the lemon juice. Cut the rest of the berries in half if desired and fold into the cooled strawberry mixture. Pour into pie shell. Refrigerate until chilled and serve with whipped cream.

NUT TORTE

Torte:

2½ cups pecans
2 tbsp. flour
6 eggs, separated
1 cup sugar
1 tsp. vanilla
1 tsp. grated orange peel

Orange icing:

½ cup butter, softened
1 cup confectioners' icing sugar
4 tbsp. orange-flavored liqueur
4 tbsp. grated orange peel

Topping:

4 cups sliced strawberries or raspberries

Preheat oven to 350 degrees. Chop nuts finely in a blender. Add the flour and mix. Beat the egg yolks until light. Gradually add the sugar and continue beating about 5 minutes. Beat in vanilla. Fold in the nut mixture and orange peel. Beat the egg whites to moist stiff peaks. Fold about ¼ of egg whites into egg yolk mixture. Fold in remaining whites until no large lumps of white remain. Pour into a greased 10-inch springform pan. Bake 45 minutes or until the center tests done. Cool on a rack. Remove the outside of the springform pan. The torte can be left on the bottom of the pan or transferred to a tray. Make orange icing by beating all ingredients together and covering the torte. At serving time, add the strawberries. (If using frozen defrosted berries, add some to each piece when serving.) Serves 12.

STRAWBERRY HAZELNUT TORTE

Torte:

8 egg whites, room temperature
2 cups sugar
1½ cups finely ground roasted hazelnuts
Butter (optional)
Cornstarch (optional)

Filling:

4 pints strawberries, rinsed, hulled, cored, and blotted dry
Sugar
1 quart heavy cream
6 tbsp. powdered sugar
¼ cup Grand Marnier
1 jar (10–12 oz.) raspberry preserves
10 fresh mint leaves for garnish (optional)

For Torte:

Preheat oven to 100 degrees. Beat egg whites until soft peaks form, 3–5 minutes. Gradually add sugar while beating continuously until egg whites are stiff and glossy, 15–20 minutes. Fold in hazelnuts and spoon into pastry bag. Pipe out three 9-inch discs that are ½-inch high onto baking sheet. Baking sheet should be lined with brown paper that is buttered and dusted with cornstarch. Smooth the meringues and bake until very lightly browned and firm to the touch, about 1–1½ hours. Cool on wire racks in dry place or dry in oven with heat turned off and door ajar.

For filling:

Reserve enough unblemished whole strawberries to top one 9-inch disc, place these in broiler pan, and sprinkle with sugar. Put under broiler for one minute to glaze. Set aside. Slice remaining strawberries into a bowl and set aside. In a separate bowl, combine cream and powdered sugar; whip until almost stiff. Add Grand Marnier and continue whipping until stiff.

Spread one third of the raspberry preserves over each meringue. Do the same with the sliced strawberries. Cover two meringue discs with whipped cream, leaving the third to top the torte. Stack the discs and cover the top one with whipped cream. Decorate it with glazed whole strawberries. Cover the sides of the torte with remaining whipped cream. Decorate with rosettes of whipped cream and mint leaves if desired.

115

STRAWBERRY CHANTILLY TORTE

1 pkg. (15.4 oz.) creamy white frosting mix
1½ cups whipping cream
1 pkg. (18.5 oz.) white cake mix
1 pint fresh strawberries, hulled and cored

Combine and refrigerate frosting mix and the whipping cream in a small mixing bowl for at least 1 hour. Bake the cake mix, following the package directions, in 2 round layer pans. Cool. Slice strawberries lengthwise and reserve ½ cup of outside slices for garnish. Split cake layers to make 4 layers. Beat frosting mixture until soft peaks form. Fill layers with ⅔ cup frosting mixture and about ½ cup strawberries. Frost the top of the cake with remaining frosting mixture and garnish with reserved berries.

Variation:
Substitute 8 ounces cream cheese, softened, and 1 tablespoon milk for the whipping cream. Add one teaspoon almond extract. Proceed as above.

STRAWBERRY GELATIN TORTE

1 pkg. (18.5 oz.) white cake mix
1 pkg. (3 oz.) strawberry gelatin
1 cup boiling water
1 pkg. (10 oz.) strawberries, slightly thawed
Whipped topping

Prepare cake and bake in two layers. Cool and place in refrigerator. Dissolve gelatin in water and add strawberries. Cool and pour in a cake pan in the same dimension as the cake layers, and place in refrigerator to set. When solid, loosen the gelatin/strawberry layer and slide onto the torte, setting the second cake layer on top. Frost with topping and refrigerate until serving time.

QUICK BERRY TORTONI

Combine crumbled macaroon cookies, Amaretto liqueur or almond extract, whipped cream, and strawberries or raspberries. Freeze until firm. Very good!

HIMMEL TORTE

1½ cups butter or margarine
¼ cup sugar
4 egg yolks
4 cups flour
1 tsp. grated lemon peel
1 egg white
¼ cup sugar
1 tsp. cinnamon
½ cup almonds, chopped

Filling:
1 cup raspberry jam
2 cups sour cream
1 tbsp. cornstarch
¼ cup sugar
2 egg yolks, well beaten
½ tsp. vanilla

Preheat oven to 450 degrees. Cream butter and sugar and beat in egg yolks one at a time. Add flour and lemon peel, and mix. Pat into two greased 10-inch pans. Brush tops with a mixture of egg white, sugar, and cinnamon. Sprinkle with almonds. Bake 10–12 minutes. If not completely baked, reduce heat to 350 degrees and bake until well browned. Cool. Spread raspberry jam over the bottom layer. Combine sour cream, cornstarch, and sugar. Cook and stir over medium heat, about 5 minutes. Gradually pour into the egg yolks. Reheat for one minute. Add vanilla. Spread ½ of the filling over the jam. Add the second layer and spread with remaining filling. Serves 12–15.

STRAWBERRY CRUMB PIE

6 cups fresh strawberries, hulled, cored, and cut in half
¾ cup sugar
¼ cup quick-cooking tapioca
1 deep-dish 9-inch pie crust
¼ cup packed light brown sugar
½ tsp. ground cinnamon

Toss strawberries with sugar and tapioca. Set aside. Prepare pastry, reserving about ½ cup pastry crumbs for topping. Fill pie crust with berry mixture. Cut an 8-inch round of foil and place over filling. Bake at 400 degrees for 35 minutes. Blend reserved flour mixture with brown sugar and cinnamon. Remove foil and sprinkle flour mixture evenly over pie. Continue baking 25 minutes or until crust and topping are browned. Serve with whipped cream.

CHOCOLATE TORTE

1 pkg. (19 oz.) lemon cake mix
2 eggs

Preheat oven to 350 degrees. Prepare cake as package directs, using 2 eggs and the amount of water specified. Pour batter into a 10 × 12-inch pan that has been greased and lined with waxed paper. Bake 20 minutes or until the surface springs back when lightly touched. Cool in pan 5 minutes, then turn onto a wire rack.

Chocolate filling:
6 oz. semisweet chocolate chips
6 oz. cream cheese, softened
3 tbsp. milk
4 cups confectioners' icing sugar
⅛ tsp. salt
1 tsp. vanilla
½ cup raspberry or strawberry jam
¼ cup slivered almonds

Melt chocolate over hot water. In medium bowl, blend cream cheese with milk. Gradually add sugar, beating until smooth. Beat in salt, vanilla, and the melted chocolate.

Cut the 10 × 15-inch cake crosswise into 4 pieces, each 10 × 3¾. Place one piece on serving plate and spread with ¼ cup jam. Top with second strip and spread with some of the chocolate filling. Top with third strip and spread with rest of jam. Top with last strip, and frost top and sides with remaining chocolate filling. Garnish with almonds. Refrigerate at least one hour before serving. Serves 12–15.

MINNIE'S CALIFORNIA STRAWBERRY PIE

1 baked pie shell, using your favorite recipe
Unblemished strawberries, washed, hulled, and cored

Coat the bottom of the pie shell with powdered sugar. Set strawberries pointed end up, filling in with halved berries. Cover with whipped cream or your favorite topping. Chill an hour before serving.

JAMS AND JELLIES

STRAWBERRY PRESERVES I

4 cups hulled strawberries
3¾ cups sugar

Put half the berries and half the sugar in a large heavy saucepan. Bring very slowly to boiling point, stirring frequently. Boil 10 minutes. Add remaining berries and sugar. Bring to boiling point and boil rapidly about 19–25 minutes or until syrup sheets from spoon, stirring occasionally to prevent sticking. Skim and pour into a bowl. Let stand overnight. Fill sterilized jars with cold preserves. Seal with hot paraffin, then cover and store. Note: For perfect results do not try to make these preserves with more than 4 cups strawberries in each batch.

STRAWBERRY PRESERVES II

1 quart strawberries
½ cup lemon juice
5 cups sugar

Put strawberries in a 2-quart saucepan. Pour lemon juice over the berries. Add 1 cup of sugar over berries and bring to a boil. Boil hard for 1 minute. Repeat this process until all sugar has been used. Then, after adding the 5th cup of sugar, cook 5 more minutes at a hard boil. May be canned hot or allowed to cool overnight. A pat of butter melted in the berries will reduce foam.

119

STRAWBERRY PRESERVES III

2 cups sugar
2 cups strawberries
2 tbsp. vinegar

Put all ingredients in heavy saucepan over medium heat. Shake until mixture begins to boil. Boil 10 minutes without stirring. Pour into a shallow 13-inch pan. Refrigerate for 24 hours before sealing in pint jar. Yield: 1 pint.

TASTY STRAWBERRY PRESERVES

3 cups sugar
1 quart strawberries
Juice of ½ lemon
1 tsp. butter

Add 2 cups sugar to berries and boil rapidly for 5 minutes. Add remaining sugar, juice of lemon, and butter. Boil 5 minutes longer. Cool 25 minutes before sealing in jars. Yield: 2 pints.

STRAWBERRY JAM

2 pints fresh strawberries
7 cups sugar
½ of 6 oz. bottle liquid fruit pectin

Wash, core, and stem berries. Slice in half lengthwise or quarter large berries. Measure 4 cups into large saucepan. Add one cup sugar, mixing carefully. Let stand 15 minutes. Add remaining sugar and mix well. Bring to a full rolling boil and boil hard one minute, stirring constantly. Remove from heat. Stir in pectin. Stir and skim alternately 5 minutes to prevent floating fruit. Ladle into hot sterilized jars. Seal at once. Makes 7 half-pint jars of jam.

STRAWBERRY JAM (AMISH)

6 cups sugar
1 cup water
2 cups strawberries, hulled
1 tsp. alum

Combine sugar and water. Boil 10 minutes. Add strawberries and boil 5 minutes longer. Add alum and boil one more minute. Pour into jars and seal.

SURE-JELL HOMEMADE STRAWBERRY JAM

2 cups mashed strawberries (about 1 quart)
1 pkg. Sure-Jell (fruit pectin)
4 cups sugar (precise measure)
¾ cup water

Stir strawberries and sugar together, mixing thoroughly. Set aside. Stir Sure-Jell and water in saucepan. Bring to a boil, stirring constantly. Boil one minute. Stir mixture together until sugar is completely dissolved and no longer grainy. Pour into containers. Cover. Let stand overnight. Store in freezer until opened. Then store in refrigerator. Makes four 8-ounce jars.

CHERRY-STRAWBERRY JAM

1 can (20 oz.) pitted tart red cherries (water pack)
1 pkg. (10 oz.) frozen sliced strawberries, thawed
4½ cups sugar
3 tbsp. lemon juice
½ of 6 oz. bottle liquid fruit pectin

Drain cherries, reserving juice. Chop cherries. Measure and add enough reserved juice to make 2 cups. Combine fruits, sugar, and lemon juice in large saucepan. Bring to a full rolling boil and boil hard one minute, stirring constantly. Remove from heat and quickly stir in pectin. Skim off foam. Stir and skim for 5 minutes. Ladle quickly into hot sterilized jars. Seal. Makes 6 half-pint jars.

FROZEN STRAWBERRY JAM

Thaw two 10-ounce packages of frozen strawberries. Put through food mill or mash. Add 3½ cups sugar and mix well. Let stand 20 minutes, stirring occasionally. When sugar has dissolved, add half of a 6-ounce bottle of liquid fruit pectin. Stir 3 minutes. Ladle into hot sterilized jars or clean freezer containers. Cover and let stand 24 hours, or until set. Seal with paraffin. Store jam up to 6 weeks in the refrigerator or up to one year in the freezer. Makes 4 half-pint jars.

STRAWBERRIES OR RASPBERRIES WITH CHAMPAGNE

1 pound strawberries or raspberries
½ cup sugar
¼ bottle (¾ cup) champagne, chilled
1 cup (½ pint) heavy cream, whipped

Wash, hull, and core strawberries, draining well. Put in glass bowl and sprinkle with sugar. Toss gently to coat. Refrigerate until chilled. Pour chilled champagne over the fruit just before serving. Serve whipped cream separately. Serves 6.

STRAWBERRY RELISH

2 quarts strawberries
1 tsp. allspice
1 tsp. cinnamon
1 tsp. cloves
7½ cups sugar
2 tbsp. vinegar
½ bottle liquid pectin

Combine all ingredients except pectin. Boil 3 minutes. Stir constantly. Remove from heat. Add pectin. Stir and skim for 5 minutes. Pour into hot sterilized jars and seal. Yield: 9½ pints.

STRAWBERRY CANDIES

1 cup ground coconut
1 cup ground pecans
2 boxes (3 oz.) strawberry gelatin
1 can Eagle Brand Condensed Milk
1 small container red sugar

Mix the coconut, pecans, and gelatin together. Add the milk and stir. The mixture will become fairly stiff. Form into small strawberries of different sizes. Roll in red sugar. Green icing can make leaves and small stems.

STRAWBERRY DIVINITY

3 cups white sugar
¾ cup water
¾ cup white syrup
2 egg whites
1 pkg. (3 oz.) strawberry gelatin
1 cup chopped nutmeats
1 tsp. vanilla

Boil together sugar, water, and syrup to hardball stage. Beat 2 egg whites until foamy. Add gelatin and continue beating until egg whites form peaks. Slowly add the sugar, water, and syrup mixture to egg whites and gelatin. Continue beating until a test spoonful will hold its shape. Add nutmeats and vanilla. Drop quickly onto waxed paper and pour in greased pan. Cut in pieces. Yields 16–20 pieces.

6. CAKES, SHORTCAKES, FROSTINGS

We will make and bake the dainty cake,
And beat the frosting light.
The sweetest bait to please a mate,
Is through the appetite.

STRAWBERRY CAKE I

1 box white cake mix
1 box (10 oz.) frozen strawberries
¾ cup oil
4 eggs
1 pkg. (3 oz.) strawberry gelatin
1 box confectioners' sugar
1 stick butter or margarine

Pour cake mix into large mixing bowl. Measure ½ cup strawberries. Fill with water to equal 1 cup. Add to mix. Add oil and mix well. Add eggs one at a time, beating well after each addition. Add strawberry gelatin and beat well. Pour into greased and floured 8 × 12-inch pan. Bake at 350 degrees until top springs back when lightly touched. Mix confectioners' sugar, butter or margarine, and remaining strawberries in mixing bowl. Spread over warm cake.

STRAWBERRY CAKE II

1 box white cake mix
½ cup frozen strawberries (not drained)
1 cup oil
½ cup boiling water
1 pkg. (6 oz.) strawberry gelatin
4 eggs

Mix all ingredients well and place in a 9 × 13-inch pan. Bake in a 350-degree oven for 30–35 minutes.

Icing:
¾ box powdered sugar
½ cup strawberries
¾ stick butter or margarine

Mix well and spready on the cooled cake.

127

STRAWBERRIES AND CREAM CAKE

2⅔ cups sifted cake flour
1½ cups sugar
2 tsp. baking powder
¼ tsp. salt
1⅓ cups heavy cream, whipped
4 eggs
1½ tsp. vanilla
Strawberry butter cream frosting

Preheat oven to 350 degrees. Grease two 9 × 1½-inch round layer cake pans. Dust lightly with flour and tap out excess. Measure flour, sugar, baking powder, and salt into a sifter. Beat cream in a medium-sized bowl until stiff and reserve. Beat eggs in a small bowl until very thick and light. Beat in vanilla. Fold into reserved whipped cream. Sift dry ingredients over cream mixture and gently fold in until batter is smooth. Pour batter in prepared pans. Bake for 30 minutes or until centers spring back when lightly pressed with fingertip. Cool layers in pans on wire racks for 10 minutes. Loosen around edges with a knife and turn out onto wire racks. Cool completely. Put layers together with strawberry butter cream frosting. Frost top and sides with remaining frosting. Garnish with strawberries if desired.

STRAWBERRY ICE BOX CAKE

1 cup strawberry puree
1 tbsp. lemon juice
2 tbsp. cold water
1 cup heavy cream
⅔ cup sugar
1 tbsp. gelatin
¼ cup boiling water
2 dozen ladyfingers

Prepare puree by rubbing fresh strawberries through a sieve or running in blender. Add sugar and lemon juice. Soften gelatin in cold water. Dissolve in boiling water and add to the strawberry mixture. Let stand until partly thickened, then fold in one half cup of the cream, whipped until stiff. Line the bottom and sides of a mold, preferably spring form, with the ladyfingers. Fill with alternate layers of the strawberry mixture and ladyfingers. Let stand in the refrigerator several hours. Whip the rest of the cream, sweetening to taste and decorate with pastry tube, as desired.

STRAWBERRY DELIGHT CAKE

48 large marshmallows
Juice of 1 lemon
1 pkg. (10 oz.) frozen sliced strawberries, thawed
2 cups whipping cream, whipped
1 commercial (8-inch) pound cake

Place marshmallows in top of a double boiler and bring water to a boil. Reduce heat to low and cook until marshmallows melt. Stir in lemon juice. Remove from heat. Add strawberries, mixing well. Fold whipped cream into the strawberry mixture.

Split the pound cake horizontally into 4 layers. Spread each layer with ⅔ cup strawberry mixture. Frost top and sides with remaining mixture. Cover and refrigerate overnight.

STRAWBERRY COFFEE CAKE

1 pkg. (8 oz.) cream cheese, softened
½ cup butter or margarine, softened
¾ cup sugar
¼ cup milk
2 eggs
1 tsp. vanilla extract
2 cups all-purpose flour
1 tsp. baking powder
½ tsp. baking soda
¼ tsp. salt
1 jar (18 oz.) strawberry preserves
1 tbsp. lemon juice
½ cup chopped pecans
¼ cup firmly packed light brown sugar

Cream the cheese and butter and gradually add ¾ cup sugar, beating until fluffy. Add milk, eggs, and vanilla: beat well. Combine flour, baking powder, soda, and salt. Add to creamed mixture and beat until blended. (Batter will be stiff.)

Spread half of batter in a greased and floured 13 × 9 × 2-inch baking pan. Combine preserves and lemon juice and spread over batter in pan. Dot remaining batter evenly over preserves. Combine pecans and brown sugar and sprinkle over top. Bake at 350 degrees for 45 minutes or until a wooden pick inserted in the center comes out clean. Yield: 15 servings.

STRAWBERRY POUND CAKE TORTE

1 all-butter cake, thawed
1 pkg. (3 oz.) vanilla pudding mix
1¼ cups milk
1½ cups sliced fresh or thawed frozen strawberries
1 cup whipping cream
2 tbsp. sugar
½ tsp. vanilla

Remove cake from foil pan and slice lengthwise in 3 layers. Prepare pudding according to package directions, using 1¼ cups milk. Cool completely. Spread half of pudding on bottom layer of cake. Arrange ½ cup strawberries on pudding. Top with middle cake layer, repeat pudding and strawberry layers. Replace top cake layer. Whip cream with sugar and vanilla and fold in remaining ½ cup strawberries. Spread on top and sides of torte. Refrigerate at least 1 hour before serving. Serves 8.

STRAWBERRY BANANA ANGEL CAKE

1 pkg. (14½ oz.) angel food cake mix
1 pkg. (3 oz.) strawberry gelatin
1 pkg. (3 oz.) banana gelatin
1 pkg. (10 oz.) frozen strawberries
2 medium-sized ripe bananas (sliced)
1 tsp. lemon juice
1 carton (8 oz.) frozen whipped topping (thawed)

Bake angel food cake according to package directions. Cool and remove from pan. Prepare gelatin according to package directions but using only 1½ cups water. Slice bananas and sprinkle with lemon juice to prevent discoloration. Reserve a few banana slices for garnish. Fold strawberries and banana slices into gelatin. Enlarge the center hole of cake by removing about 1 inch with a sharp knife. Tear this removed cake* into small pieces and fold into gelatin. Place whole cake on serving platter. Fill the hole of the cake with gelatin. Frost top and sides with the thawed whipped topping and garnish with the reserved banana slices.

*Note: Freezing the cake pieces first before adding to gelatin mixture prevents loss of volume.

DANISH STRAWBERRY CAKE

Pastry:

1 cup flour
6 tbsp. butter, room temperature
6 tbsp. confectioners' sugar
1 egg yolk
½ tsp. vanilla

Filling:

1 cup currant jelly
1 quart fresh strawberries, hulled and cored
1 cup heavy cream, whipped

Preheat oven to 375 degrees. To make pastry, sift flour onto a pastry board and make a well in the center of the flour. Put into it the butter, confectioner's sugar, egg yolk, and vanilla. Work mixture with your hands into a smooth dough. Set aside in refrigerator to chill. Roll dough into a circle (or oblong) ¼-inch thick. Pinch the edge to decorate and prick the center with a fork. Place dough on greased baking sheet and bake for 12–15 minutes. Cool on a wire rack.

To make the filling, heat the jelly in a small saucepan and brush jelly over the pastry shell. Arrange whole strawberries on pastry and brush with remaining jelly. Before serving, decorate with rosettes of whipped cream or pass whipped cream separately.

Note: Pastry stores well and can be made ahead of time. Also, other fruits such as raspberries, sweet cherries, drained canned apricots, pineapple, and grapes may be used. Glaze red fruit with red jelly and yellow fruit with light-colored jam or jelly.

ANGEL STRAWBERRY DELIGHT

1 angel food cake (commercial or homemade)
1 quart fresh strawberries, hulled and cored
1 large container dessert topping
2 cups heavy cream, whipped

Mix together dessert topping and the whipped cream. Remove half of it (2–3 cups) for use later. Slice the strawberries, reserving ten whole ones for garnish. Add a little sugar, if desired, to the sliced strawberries. Divide the angel food cake in half crosswise. Mix sliced strawberries with half of the whipped topping and spread on bottom layer of cake. Replace the top half of cake and frost the cake with the reserved topping. Decorate the top of the cake with the whole strawberries. Keep refrigerated until ready to serve.

STRAWBERRY-RHUBARB COFFEE CAKE

Filling: (Prepare first so it can cool.)
3 cups frozen sliced strawberries, thawed
3 cups frozen diced rhubarb
2 tbsp. lemon juice
1 cup sugar
⅓ cup cornstarch

Combine strawberries and rhubarb in a saucepan. Cover and cook about 5 minutes. Add lemon juice, sugar, and cornstarch and cook until thick. Cool.

Topping:
¾ cup sugar
½ cup flour
¼ cup butter or margarine

Combine sugar and flour. Cut in butter to make fine crumbs.

Batter:
3 cups flour
1 cup sugar
1 tsp. baking soda
1 tsp. baking powder
1 tsp. salt
1 cup butter or margarine
1 cup buttermilk
2 eggs, slightly beaten
1 tsp. vanilla

Preheat oven to 350 degrees. Sift together flour, sugar, soda, baking powder, and salt. Cut in butter to make fine crumbs. Beat together the buttermilk, eggs, and vanilla. Add to dry ingredients and stir until just moistened. Spread ½ of the batter in a greased 9 × 13-inch pan. Carefully spread strawberry-rhubarb filling over batter. Spoon remaining batter in small mounds over filling. Sprinkle topping over all. Bake 40–45 minutes. Serves 12–15.

STRAWBERRY CAKE ROLL

4 eggs, separated
¾ cup sugar
1 tsp. vanilla extract
¾ cup sifted cake flour
¾ tsp. baking powder
¼ tsp. salt
Powdered sugar

1 cup whipping cream
3 tbsp. sugar
¼ tsp. vanilla extract
1 pkg. (10 oz.) frozen sliced strawberries,
*   drained*
¼ cup strawberry jam
¼ cup light corn syrup

Grease a 15 × 10 × ½-inch jelly roll pan and line with waxed paper. Grease and flour waxed paper; set aside. Beat egg yolks until thick and lemon-colored. Gradually add ¾ cup sugar, beating well. Stir in 1 teaspoon vanilla. Combine flour and baking powder and gradually add to sugar mixture, beating just until blended. Beat egg whites (at room temperture) and salt until stiff peaks form. Stir one fourth of egg white mixture into flour mixture. Repeat with remaining egg white mixture, stirring in one third of mixture at a time. Spread batter evenly in prepared pan. Bake at 375 degrees for 10 to 12 minutes.

Sift powdered sugar in a 15 × 10-inch rectangle on a towel. When cake is done, immediately loosen from sides of pan and turn out onto powdered sugar. Peel off waxed paper. Starting at the short edge, roll up cake and towel together. Cool cake on a wire rack, seam side down.

Beat whipping cream until foamy. Gradually add 3 tablespoons sugar, beating until soft peaks form. Add ¼ teaspoon vanilla; beat until blended. Fold in strawberries. Unroll cake and remove towel. Spread cake with strawberry filling and reroll. Place on serving plate, seam side down. Combine jam and corn syrup in a small saucepan. Bring to a boil, stirring constantly. Remove from heat and brush mixture over cake roll. Chill until serving time. Serves 8–10.

STRAWBERRY GLAZED CHEESE CAKE

Crust:

¾ cup coarsely ground walnuts (3 oz.)
¾ cup finely crushed graham crackers
3 tbsp. melted unsalted butter

Preheat oven to 350 degrees. Lightly butter springform pan. Combine walnuts, crumbs, and butter. Press into bottom of pan.

Filling:

4 pkgs. (8 oz. each) cream cheese, room temperature
4 eggs
1¼ cups sugar
1 tbsp. fresh lemon juice
2 tsp. vanilla

Beat cream cheese in large bowl. Add eggs, sugar, lemon juice, and vanilla. Spoon over crust. Set pan on baking sheet. Bake 10-inch cake 40-45 minutes. Bake 9-inch cake 50-55 minutes. Remove from oven and let stand at room temperature for 15 minutes. Retain oven temperature at 350 degrees.

Topping:

2 cup sour cream
¼ cup sugar
1 tsp. vanilla

Combine sour cream, sugar, and vanilla. Cover and refrigerate. When cake has finished baking, spoon topping over, starting at center and extending to within ½-inch of edge. Return to oven and bake 5 minutes more. Let cool and then refrigerate at least 24 hours.

Glaze:

1 quart medium-sized strawberries
1 jar (12 oz.) red raspberry jelly
1 tbsp. cornstarch
¼ cup Cointreau
¼ cup water

Prepare berries and dry completely on paper towels. Combine a little jelly with cornstarch in saucepan and mix well. Add remaining jelly, Cointreau, and water. Cook over medium heat, stirring frequently, until thickened and clear, about 5 minutes. Cool to lukewarm, stirring occasionally. Using knife, loosen cake from pan. Remove from springform. Arrange berries pointed ends up over cake. Spoon glaze over berries, allowing some to drip down sides. Return to refrigerator until glaze is set.

PAN SHORTCAKE

2 eggs, separated
1 cup sugar
⅓ cup hot water
¼ tsp. lemon juice
1 cup cake flour, sifted
1½ tsp. baking powder
¼ tsp. salt

Filling:

4 cups fresh sliced strawberries or raspberries, thawed and drained
1 cup juice from berries
2 tbsp. cornstarch
½ tsp. almond extract

Meringue:

4 egg whites
½ tsp. cream of tartar
½ cup sugar

Preheat oven to 325 degrees. Beat yolks until thick and lemon colored. Gradually beat in remaining sugar. Fold egg whites into egg yolk mixture. Fold in the sifted dry ingredients. Pour batter into greased 9 × 13-inch pan. Bake about 35 minutes. Cool. Cover the cake with fresh berries. If using frozen berries, cook the juice and cornstarch until mixture thickens. Add almond extract and berries and spoon over cake. Preheat oven to 375 degrees. Prepare the meringue by beating the egg whites and cream of tartar until foamy and gradually adding, while beating, the sugar. Beat until stiff peaks form. Cover the cake with meringue and brown in oven 3–5 minutes or as desired.

STRAWBERRY SHORTCAKES

1 quart strawberries, hulled, cored, and sliced
1 cup sugar
½ cup shortening
2 cups all-purpose flour
2 tbsp. sugar
3 tsp. baking powder
1 tsp. salt
½ cup milk
Butter or margarine, softened
Sweetened whipped cream

Mix strawberries with 1 cup sugar. Let stand 1 hour.

Heat oven to 450 degrees. Cut shortening into flour, 2 tablespoons sugar, baking powder, and salt, combined, until mixture resembles fine crumbs. Stir in milk just until blended. Gently smooth dough into a ball on lightly floured cloth-covered board. Knead 20–25 times. Roll to ½-inch thickness. Cut with floured 3-inch cutter. Place about 1-inch apart on ungreased cookie sheet.

Bake until golden brown, 10–12 minutes. Split in two while hot. Spread with butter or margarine. Fill and top with strawberries and whipped cream. Serves 6.

Note: Recipe may also be baked in an 8-inch square pan and cut in 6 squares. These squares may be split in half and filled and topped with strawberries and whipped cream.

DOUBLE SHORTCAKE

⅓ cup brown sugar
1 tbsp. grated orange peel
3 cups flour, sifted
4 tsp. baking powder
1 tsp. salt
¾ cup butter or margarine
¾ cup milk
3 cups ice cream of choice
3 cups strawberries or raspberries

Preheat oven to 450 degrees. Combine brown sugar and orange peel. In another bowl, combine flour, baking powder, and salt. Add ½ of brown sugar mixture. Cut in butter to resemble fine meal. Add milk and combine until just blended. Pat ½ of dough into greased round 9-inch pan. Drop remaining dough on an inverted round 8-inch pan. Make 8 equal mounds in a circle around the outer edge of the pan. Sprinkle tops with remaining brown sugar mixture. Bake 10–25 minutes. Spread ice cream over the 9-inch shortcake. Add layer of berries and top with circle of biscuits. Fill center with berries. Serves 8.

MUFFIN SHORTCAKE

4 cups strawberries or raspberries
¼ cup honey
1 tsp. grated lemon peel

Sauce:
1 cup sour cream
3 tbsp. honey

Shortcake:
1½ cups flour, unsifted
½ cup sugar
1 tbsp. poppy seed
2 tsp. baking powder
½ tsp. salt
¼ cup shortening
1 egg, beaten
¾ cup milk

Carefully combine the berries, honey, and lemon peel and let stand while preparing the sauce and shortcake.

Stir together the sour cream and honey until just blended.

Preheat oven to 400 degrees. Grease twelve 2½ × 1¼-inch muffin cups.

Combine flour, sugar, poppy seed, baking powder, and salt. Cut in shortening until mixture resembles coarse crumbs. Combine beaten egg and milk and add to flour mixture. Stir with fork until just moistened. Spoon into prepared muffin cups. Bakea bout 20 minutes. Split warm muffins. Cover with berry mixture and top with sour cream mixture. Serves 12.

137

PECAN STRAWBERRY SHORTCAKE

Makes 8–10 individual servings or one large shortcake.

2 cups all-purpose flour
½ cup finely ground pecans
¼ cup sugar
2 tsp. baking powder
½ cup butter or margarine
1 beaten egg
⅔ cup milk
3 tsp. finely shredded orange peel

6 cups sliced fresh strawberries
¼ cup sugar
1 cup whipping cream
2 tbsp. sugar
½ tsp. vanilla
Whole strawberries (optional)

In a medium mixing bowl, stir together flour, ground pecans, the first ¼ cup sugar, and baking powder. Cut in butter or margarine until the mixture resembles coarse crumbs.

In a mixing bowl, combine egg, milk, and 2 teaspoons of the orange peel. Add all at once to dry ingredients. Stir just until moistened. Drop the dough into 8–10 mounds on an ungreased baking sheet. Flatten each mound with the back of a spoon until about ¾-inch thick. Bake in a 450-degree oven for 7–8 minutes or until golden. Transfer shortcakes to a wire rack. Cool about 10 minutes.

Meanwhile, in a bowl stir together berries, the second ¼ cup of sugar, and the remaining one teaspoon of orange peel. Let stand about 20 minutes.

To whip cream: In a chilled medium mixing bowl, combine the whipping cream, the 2 tablespoons sugar, and vanilla. Beat with the chilled beaters of an electric mixer on medium speed until soft peaks form.

Using a sharp serrated knife, cut each shortcake in half horizontally. Carefully lift off layers. Spoon half the strawberries and half the whipped cream over the bottom layers. Replace shortcake tops. Top with remaining strawberries, then spoon remaining cream directly into strawberries. Top with a strawberry. Serve immediately. Serves 8–10.

For a large shortcake:
Grease an 8-inch × 1½-inch round baking pan and set aside. Prepare shortcake

dough as directed. Use a rubber spatula to spread dough in the prepared pan, and build up edges slightly so the cake rises to the same height all around. Bake in a 450-degree oven for 15–18 minutes or until a toothpick inserted in the center comes out clean (do not overbake). Cool shortcake in pan on a wire rack for 10 minutes. Remove from pan.

Using a long serrated knife, cut shortcake in half horizontally. Using a wide spatula or inserting a sheet of waxed paper, carefully lift off the tender top layer of shortcake. Spoon half the strawberries over bottom layer, then about half the whipped cream. Replace shortcake top. Add remaining strawberries, then spoon remaining cream directly into strawberries. Top with a whole strawberry, cut and fanned, and chopped pecans. Serve immediately. Serves 8–10.

SHORTCAKE WITH NUTS

Shortcake:
3 cups flour
½ cup sugar
1 tsp. salt
4 tsp. baking powder
½ tsp. nutmeg
½ tsp. cinnamon
½ tsp. cardamon
¾ cup butter
1 cup finely chopped pecans or walnuts
2 egg yolks
⅔ cup milk

Filling:
4 cups strawberries
¾ cup sugar
2 egg whites
1 cup whipping cream

Preheat oven to 450 degrees. Sift flour, sugar, salt, baking powder, and spices together. Rub butter into flour until it resembles fine bread crumbs. Add nuts. Beat egg yolks and milk together. Add to flour mixture. Knead a few times on lightly floured board. Divide dough into 3 pieces. Press each piece into 8-inch cake pan. Bake 12–15 minutes until golden brown. Turn out and cool on wire rack. Prepare filling.

Combine strawberries and sugar and set aside. Beat egg whites stiff. Whip the cream and fold into stiffly beaten egg whites. Divide strawberries and whipped cream mixture between layers and on top of shortcake. Serves 6–8.

CHOCOLATE STRAWBERRY SHORTCAKE

6 cups fresh strawberries
¾ cup sugar
1⅔ cups all-purpose flour
⅓ cup cocoa
1 tbsp. baking powder
¼ tsp. salt
½ cup butter or margarine
⅔ cup milk
1 egg, beaten
1 cup cold whipping cream
2 tbsp. powdered sugar

Reserve six strawberries. Slice remaining berries. In bowl, gently stir together sliced berries and ¼ cup of the sugar; set aside. Preheat oven to 450 degrees. Grease an 8-inch round baking pan. In a separated bowl, stir together flour, cocoa, remaining ½ cup sugar, baking powder, and salt. Cut in butter until mixture resembles coarse crumbs. In a separate bowl, stir together milk and egg. Add all at once to dry ingredients, stirring just until moistened. Spread dough in prepared pan, building up edges slightly. Bake in a 450-degree oven for 15–18 minutes, or until wooden pick inserted in center comes out clean. Cool 10 minutes. Remove from pan and place on serving plate.

In a small mixing bowl, beat whipping cream and powdered sugar until stiff. Arrange some sliced berries over the cake and top with whipped cream. Garnish with reserved whole strawberries. Serve shortcake with remaining sliced berries. Serves 8.

STRAWBERRY SHORTCAKE TRIFLE

1 pint fresh strawberries
2 tbsp. sugar
2 cups vanilla pudding
1 pkg. (3 oz.) cream cheese
2 cups shortcake or pound cake cubes

Slice 1 cup berries and arrange around the sides of a clear dish. Puree the remaining berries with sugar. Mix pudding with the cream cheese. Place ½ of cake in bottom of dish. Layer ½ of pureed berries over cake, then ½ of pudding. Repeat until all is used. Chill 24 hours. Serves 6–8.

SHORTCAKE BISCUITS AND STRAWBERRIES

2 cups flour
1 tbsp. baking powder
3 tbsp. sugar
½ tsp. salt
½ cup chilled butter, cut in small pieces, or
  ¼ cup solid vegetable shortening and ¼ cup butter
⅔ cup milk or half-and-half
1–2 tbsp. soft butter
1 cup whipping cream
2 tbsp. sifted confectioners' sugar
⅛ tsp. freshly grated nutmeg

6 cups fresh strawberries, hulled and cored
3 tbsp. sugar
1 tbsp. strawberry liqueur

Preheat oven to 423 degrees and lightly grease a cookie sheet. To make the biscuits, sift together flour, baking powder, sugar, and salt into a bowl. Blend with pastry blender or with fingertips until the mixture has the consistency of coarse crumbs. Add the milk all at once and stir with a fork until the dough just comes together.

Turn dough out on a lightly floured pastry cloth or board. Knead lightly about 12–15 times, sprinkling with a little flour if dough gets sticky. Roll out or pat the dough into a rectangle ½-inch thick. Cut into rounds with a floured 3-inch biscuit cutter or cut into squares with a knife. Cool enough to handle and split in two, buttering the bottom half before placing in individual serving dishes. Spoon prepared strawberries over the bottom and top halves, and finish with desired amount of whipped cream or dessert topping.

141

AMERICAN FLAG SHORTCAKE

4 cups flour
8 tsp. baking powder
1 tsp. cream of tartar
1 tsp. salt
¼ cup sugar
1 cup butter or margarine
1⅓ cups milk

Preheat oven to 450 degrees. Sift together flour, baking powder, cream of tartar, salt, and sugar. Cut in butter. Add milk all at once. Stir in quickly. Turn onto flour-sprinkled board. Knead a few times. Pat into a 9 × 13-inch pan. Bake about 20 minutes. Cool. Decorate with American flag designs.

Icing:
2 cups whipping cream
2 cups blueberries
8 cups strawberries, halved

Place shortcake on serving tray. Whip the cream and sweeten to taste. Cover shortcake with whipped cream. Measure a box 4½ inches deep by 5½ inches across in the upper left-hand corner. Fill in this "star field" with blueberries. Make stripe No. 1 across top of cake with strawberries. Stripe No. 4 will be parallel to bottom of the blueberry "box." Stripe No. 7 will be across the bottom of the shortcake. Fill in stripes 2, 3, 5, and 6. Serve with additional strawberries and whipped cream if desired. Raspberries could be used in place of strawberries.

FROSTINGS

VANILLA BUTTER CREAM FROSTING

½ cup (1 stick) butter or margarine
1 pkg. (1 pound) confectioners' sugar
4 tbsp. milk
2 tsp. vanilla

Beat butter or margarine in a medium-sized bowl with electric mixer until soft. Beat in sugar alternately with milk and vanilla (combined) until smooth and spreadable. Will fill and frost two 8-inch or two 9-inch cake layers.

142

Strawberry Butter Cream:

Follow basic recipe, omitting milk and vanilla. Mash enough fresh, hulled, and cored strawberries to measure ⅓ cup. Add mashed strawberries and sugar alternately with butter.

STRAWBERRY BUTTER CREAM ICING

⅓ cup soft butter
3 cups confectioners' icing sugar, sifted
3–4 tbsp. crushed fresh or frozen (thawed) strawberries

Blend together the butter and icing sugar. Stir in crushed strawberries. Yields two 9-inch layers or one 9 × 13-inch pan.

STRAWBERRY GLAZE FROSTING

1 pkg. (10 oz.) frozen strawberries
⅓ cup shortening
1 tbsp. water
1 box powdered sugar
1 tbsp. granulated sugar
1 tbsp. cornstarch

Combine melted shortening with powdered sugar. Add just enough scalded milk to make it easy to spread. Spread frosting on cake.

Put granulated sugar, cornstarch, and water in pan. Add strawberries. Heat until chalky white color becomes pink. Spread while still hot over the frosted cake. This will be enough for a 9 × 13-inch cake.

7. ICE CREAM, SHERBETS, FROZEN DESSERTS, TARTS

If each day is hemmed by prayer,
It will not unravel overnight.

STRAWBERRY ICE CREAM I

⅔ cup evaporated milk
1 pkg. (10 oz.) frozen strawberries, thawed
¼ cup sugar
Dash of salt
1 tbsp. lemon juice

Put the milk in an ice cube tray and chill in refrigerator until crystals begin to form. Meanwhile, mix strawberries, sugar, and salt together. Let stand. Put ice cold milk into a cold quart bowl. Whip with electric beater at high speed until fluffy. Add lemon juice and beat until stiff. Add strawberry mixture gradually, beating at low speed until well blended. Put into 1-quart ice tray and freeze until firm without stirring. Makes 1 quart.

STRAWBERRY ICE CREAM II

⅔ cup sweetened condensed milk
½ cup water
1 cup crushed fresh strawberries
¼ cup sugar
1 cup heavy cream

Combine milk and water. Sweeten berries to taste and stir into milk mixture. Chill in refrigerator. Whip the cream to soft custard consistency, fold into chilled mixture, and turn into ice cube tray. Freeze to firm mush (about 1 hour). Turn into a chilled bowl, then break into pieces. Whip until fluffy but not melted. Quickly return to tray. Cover the tray, return to freezer, and let freeze to firm stage. Makes 1½ pints.

147

STRAWBERRY ICE CREAM III

1 pint strawberries, plus 6–8 berries for garnish
¾ cup confectioners' sugar
Squeeze of lemon juice
¾ cup heavy cream
½ cup light cream

Wash, hull, and core strawberries, draining in a colander, and cut in small pieces. Put in blender with sieved sugar and lemon juice. Combine the two creams and whip until thick but not stiff, then blend into the strawberry puree. Spoon mixture into a plastic freezer container and cover with the lid. Put in freezer for 12 hours. One or two hours before serving, transfer the ice cream to the refrigerator to thaw slightly. Scoop the ice cream into dessert bowls and decorate with slices of fresh strawberries. Serves 6.

FRENCH STRAWBERRY ICE CREAM

1 pint strawberries, mashed with ½ cup sugar
1 cup milk
½ cup sugar
¼ tsp. salt
3 egg yolks, beaten
1 tsp. vanilla
2 cups chilled whipping cream

Mix milk, sugar, salt, and egg yolks in a saucepan. Cook over medium heat, stirring constantly, until bubbles appear around the edge. Cool to room temperature and stir in vanilla. Pour the milk mixture into an ice cube tray and freeze until it is mushy and partially frozen, 30–60 minutes. Then place mixture in a bowl and beat until smooth. Beat whipping cream in a chilled bowl until soft peaks form and carefully fold into the milk mixture. Add mashed strawberries and pour into 2 ice cube trays. Cover to prevent crystals from forming and freeze, stirring often the first several hours. Continue freezing until the ice cream is firm, about 3–4 hours. Makes 1 quart.

STRAWBERRY GELATIN ICE CREAM

2 envelopes unflavored gelatin
½ cup cold water
2 cups instant nonfat dry milk crystals
1 quart whole milk
2 cups sugar
1 pint fresh strawberries

Sprinkle gelatin over water to soften. Stir powdered milk crystals into whole milk. Blend in softened gelatin and sugar. Stir over low heat until gelatin dissolves. Cool. Meanwhile, place strawberries in a blender. Sieve the puree and stir it into the gelatin mixture. Turn into refrigerator trays and freeze until firm, then beat until smooth. Serve with additional strawberries if desired. Makes 1 quart.

EASY STRAWBERRY ICE CREAM

1 pkg. (10 oz.) sliced frozen strawberries
1 cup sugar
2 cups sour cream

Add sugar and sour cream to partially thawed strawberries and combine thoroughly. Place in freezer and stir three times at 25-minute intervals to prevent crystals from forming. Serves 4–6.

HOW TO FREEZE ICE CREAM

1. Use a stabilizer to prevent crystals from forming (an ingredient such as gelatin, eggs, flour, or cornstarch.)

2. Set control for fast freezing. Pour ice cream mixture into refrigerator tray. Place in bottom of freezing compartment.

3. To make creamy ice cream: After first mixture has partially frozen (½ hour), turn into chilled bowl. Beat with cold rotary beater until smooth (not melted). Fold in whipped cream. Return to cold refrigerator tray. Freeze until firm, stirring occasionally. Time depends on formula, temperature, etc.

149

FRESH STRAWBERRY ICE CREAM

American type:

1 cup rich milk
½ cup sugar
⅛ tsp. salt
1 tbsp. flour
1 cup whipping cream
3 tsp. vanilla (not imitation)
1½ cups mashed strawberries
½ to ¾ cup sugar

French type:

1 cup rich milk
½ cup sugar
⅛ tsp. salt
3 egg yolks, beaten
1 cup whipping cream
3 tsp. vanilla (not imitation)
1½ cups mashed strawberries
½ to ¾ cup sugar

Scald milk, gradually stir in sugar, salt, flour, and if French type, the egg yolks. Cook over low heat, stirring, until it boils. Boil just one minute. Cool. Before freezing, blend in 1½ cups mashed fresh strawberries, sweetened with ½ to ¾ cup sugar. Pour into freezer tray. Freeze ½ hour.

Whip cream until barely stiff, then beat in vanilla. Turn the partially frozen mixture into a chilled bowl. Beat with a rotary beater until smooth. Fold in whipped cream, return to cold tray, and freeze until firm, stirring well during the first hour of the freezing period.

STRAWBERRIES JUBILEE

1 pkg. (16 oz.) frozen strawberries, thawed and drained (reserve syrup)
2 tsp. cornstarch
2–3 tbsp. brandy
Vanilla ice cream

Blend reserved strawberry syrup and cornstarch. Heat over medium heat, stirring frequently, until thick and clear. Remove from heat and stir in strawberries. Pour into a chafing dish to keep warm. Heat the brandy until just warm in a long-handled ladle or small pan. Ignite and carefully pour flaming over strawberry mixture in chafing dish. Stir. Spoon over vanilla ice cream or serve with Strawberry Alaska Jubilee.

STRAWBERRY ICE MILK

2 cups sugar
¼ cup cornstarch
¼ tsp. salt
2 quarts skim milk
3 eggs, beaten
1 tbsp. unflavored gelatin
1½ tbsp. vanilla (not imitation)
2 cups strawberries, pureed (may substitute other fruit)

Mix sugar, cornstarch, and salt in top of double boiler. Blend in 4 cups milk gradually. Cook over hot water, stirring occasionally until thickened, 12–15 minutes. Stir a little of the hot cornstarch mixture into the eggs before combining with the rest of the beaten eggs. Cook over hot water, stirring, until mixture is like a soft custard. Soften gelatin in one cup skim milk and stir into hot mixture. Chill thoroughly to ensure a smooth ice milk. Stir in vanilla and remaining 3 cups skim milk. Pour into a 1-gallon freezer canister (not more than ⅔ full) to freeze.

STRAWBERRY ICE CREAM DESSERT

2 tsp. gelatin
1 cup cold water
¾ cup nonfat dry milk
1½ cups milk
3 tbsp. sugar
1   tbsp. liquid sweetener
2 tsp. vanilla (not imitation)
1½ cups mashed strawberries
2 tbsp. lemon juice

Soften gelatin in ½ cup water. Mix ¼ cup dry milk with the milk and then scald. Dissolve gelatin in it and stir in 2 tablespoons sugar, the liquid sweetener, and vanilla. Chill until slightly thickened. Place in coldest part of freezer, stirring occasionally, for about ½ hour. Add mashed strawberries to the cooled gelatin mixture. Beat remaining ½ cup water and ½ cup dry milk until it begins to thicken. Add lemon juice and beat until thick. Beat in sugar and continue beating until mixture reaches the consistency of whipped cream. Fold in the chilled gelatin mixture. Freeze. Serves 8.

STRAWBERRY ALASKA JUBILEE

2 quarts strawberry ice cream, softened
1 pkg. (18.5 oz.) yellow cake mix
6 egg whites
½ tsp. cream of tartar
1 cup sugar
Strawberries Jubilee (see above)

Line a 1½-quart bowl with aluminum foil and pack with the ice cream. Freeze until firm. Bake the cake mix in two round layer pans, 9 × 1½ inches, according to directions on package. Cool completely. (Reserve one layer for another dessert.)

Cover a baking sheet with aluminum foil and place the cake layer on the sheet. Invert the bowl with ice cream on the cake; remove bowl and foil. Place cake and ice cream in freezer while preparing meringue. (Ice cream must be very hard before it is covered with meringue.)

Move oven rack to lowest position. Heat the oven to 500 degrees. Beat egg whites and cream of tartar until foamy. Beat in sugar, one tablespoon at a time, and continue beating until stiff and glossy. Do not underbeat. Completely cover the cake and ice cream with meringue, sealing it to foil. Bake until the meringue is light brown, 3–5 minutes. Trim foil to edge of meringue. Transfer cake to serving plate. Let stand 10–15 minutes before serving to make cutting easier. Serve with Strawberries Jubilee. Serves 12–16. Note: Dessert can be frozen up to 24 hours before or after baking meringue.

STRAWBERRY SHERBET I

2 cups strawberries, crushed
1 cup ice water
1 tsp. lemon juice and rind of 1 lemon
1½ tsp. liquid sweetener

Combine all ingredients and blend thoroughly. Freeze until mushy. Beat until fluffy. Repeat this procedure once more. Refreeze until firm. Serves 6.

STRAWBERRY SHERBET II

4 quarts fresh strawberries, hulled, cored, and sliced
4 cups sugar
3 cups milk
½ cup fresh orange juice
Rind of ½ lemon
Pinch cinnamon

Mix strawberries and sugar. Place in refrigerator for 1½ hours. Blend strawberries in blender and strain. Add remaining ingredients and pour into a large cake pan or refrigerator trays. Place in freezer. Stir periodically during the freezing process. When thick, pack in containers and store in freezer until serving time. Makes 2 quarts.

CRÈME DE MENTHE SHERBET WITH STRAWBERRIES

3 pints lemon sherbet
⅓ cup crème de menthe
2 pints fresh strawberries, washed and chilled
Superfine sugar

Let sherbet soften slightly in refrigerator for about 30 minutes. Turn sherbet into a large bowl and beat with an electric hand mixer just until smooth and softened, but do not let it melt. Quickly stir in crème de menthe until well combined. Turn into a 6-cup decorative mold. Freeze until very firm, about 24 hours. To serve, invert mold over a chilled serving plate. Place a hot damp cloth over the mold and shake out sherbet. Dust strawberries with sugar if they are too tart for your taste. Garnish sherbet with some of the strawberries and serve the remaining berries in a bowl on the side.

STRAWBERRY ICE I

1 pkg. (3 oz.) strawberry gelatin
½ cup sugar
1½ cups boiling water
1 pkg. (16 oz.) frozen sliced strawberries, partially thawed
¼ cup orange juice
¼ cup lemon juice

Blend gelatin and sugar. Pour boiling water on gelatin mixture in large bowl, stirring until gelatin is dissolved. Stir in remaining ingredients. Pour into 2 refrigerator trays and freeze until mushy, about 1 hour. Remove from trays and beat until smooth. Return to trays and freeze until firm (about 1 hour). Serves 8–10.

STRAWBERRY ICE II

1 pint strawberries, hulled and cored, and thoroughly drained
¼ cup confectioners' sugar
2 cups lemonade
2 egg whites

Cut strawberries in small pieces. Put strawberries and sugar in a blender and blend to make a puree. Add enough lemonade to the strawberry puree to make 2 cups liquid. Spoon the mixture into an ice cube tray. Cover with foil and freeze. When mixture begins to freeze around the sides of the container, remove from the freezer. Scrape the frozen bits into the center with a fork to break up any ice crystals. Whip the egg whites until stiff but not dry and fold them into the strawberry mixture. Return to the freezer or spoon into small molds. Cover and freeze the ice until set.

STRAWBERRY ICE III

2 cups fresh strawberries
¼ cup sugar
½ cup water
2 tbsp. unsweetened orange juice
2 egg whites
¼ tsp. cream of tartar
Pinch of salt

Combine strawberries, sugar, water, and orange juice in a blender. Blend until smooth. Pour the mixture into a medium saucepan, and cook over low heat 5 minutes, stirring occasionally. Let cool and pour into a medium mixing bowl. Freeze 45 minutes or until slushy. Combine egg whites (at room temperature), cream of tartar, and salt in mixing bowl. Beat until soft peaks form. Beat the strawberry mixture until fluffy and smooth. Fold in egg whites. Freeze until firm. Serves 6 (about 57 calories per serving).

TANGY STRAWBERRY POPS

1 pkg. (10 oz.) sliced strawberries, thawed
¾ cup sugar
2 cups buttermilk
½ tsp. vanilla (not imitation)
2 egg whites, stiffly beaten

Heat strawberries until warm. Add sugar and stir until dissolved. Cool. Add remaining ingredients and fold in carefully. Pour into small paper cups or other containers. Freeze. When partly frozen, place a wooden stick in the center of each pop.

STRAWBERRY ICE (OR OTHER FRUIT)

3 lbs. strawberries, hulled and cored
1½ cups superfine sugar

Strawberries are to be well drained after rinsing. If using other fruits such as peaches, peel and remove pits. Weigh the fruit to be sure there are three pounds. Put fruit in a blender or food processor and blend to a fine puree. (This makes about 6 cups.)

Transfer puree to a large mixing bowl. Add the sugar, one cup at a time, and blend well. (You may want to increase or decrease sugar, depending on sweetness of fruit.) Put the mixture in an electric ice cream freezer and freeze according to manufacturer's directions. Serves 12.

STRAWBERRY PARFAIT I

1 quart strawberries, mashed
2 cups sugar
½ cup water
3 egg whites, beaten stiff
2 cups cream, whipped

Stir one cup of the sugar into strawberries and let stand 2 hours. Strain. Freeze strawberries until icy. Combine the remaining cup of sugar and water and boil for 5 minutes. Beat this syrup into the egg whites and continue beating until the mixture is cool. Fold all ingredients together and freeze until firm.

STRAWBERRY PARFAIT II

½ cup sugar
¼ cup water
1 tbsp. orange juice
1 cup strawberries, crushed
1 cup cream, whipped
2 egg whites, beaten stiff

Boil sugar and water for 5 minutes. Add strawberries. Cook in a double boiler, stirring until thick, about 15 minutes. Add orange juice. Cool. Fold in whipped cream and egg whites. Freeze until firm.

STRAWBERRY MALLOW PARFAIT

1 cup strawberries, crushed (or other fruit)
2 tbsp. lemon juice
½ pound cut-up marshmallows
1 cup cream, whipped
2 egg whites, beaten stiff
2 tbsp. sugar

Heat strawberries, marshmallows, and lemon juice. Stir until smooth and creamy. Cool. Add sugar to beaten egg whites. Beat until thoroughly blended. Fold all ingredients together and freeze.

STRAWBERRY MOUSSE I

2 pkgs. (10 oz.) frozen strawberries
⅔ cup corn syrup
⅓ cup sugar
⅓ cup water
3 egg whites
1½ tsp. vanilla (not imitation)
3 egg yolks
2 cups heavy cream, whipped

Thaw strawberries. Combine corn syrup, sugar, and water in a saucepan. Bring to a boil and boil for 2 minutes. Beat the egg whites until stiff but not dry. Gradually beat in hot syrup, continuing until mixture is thick and creamy. Add vanilla. Beat egg yolks until thick and fold into egg whites. Fold in cream and strawberries. Pour into freezing trays lined with aluminum foil or into a 2-quart mold. Freeze without stirring. Then turn out of trays, remove foil, and cut into blocks. Or, to remove mousse from mold, cover outside of mold for a few seconds with a cloth wrung out of hot water.

STRAWBERRY MOUSSE II

⅔ cup crushed strawberries, sweetened to taste
1½ cups cream, whipped
⅔ cup sweetened condensed milk
½ tsp. lemon rind

Combine all ingredients, blending thoroughly. Freeze until firm.

STRAWBERRY YOGURT MOUSSE

1 cup crushed strawberries
1 cup strawberry yogurt
1 cup heavy cream, whipped
2 tbsp. sugar
1 egg white
2 tbsp. sugar

Beat egg white until stiff. Add 2 tablespoons sugar and whipped cream. Mix until well blended. Stir in yogurt, strawberries, and remaining sugar. Freeze until firm.

FROZEN STRAWBERRY YOGURT DESSERT

Pastry:

1½ cups flour
1 cup butter or margarine, softened
½ cup powdered sugar

Heat oven to 400 degrees. Combine the pastry ingredients and spread in ungreased rectangular pan 13 × 9 × 2. Bake until edges are golden, 12–15 minutes. Cool.

Topping:

2 cups chilled whipping cream
¼ cup powdered sugar
1 carton (8 oz.) strawberry yogurt
1 pkg. (10 oz.) frozen strawberries, partially thawed

In a chilled large bowl, beat the cream and powdered sugar until stiff. Fold yogurt and strawberries into the whipped cream. Spoon over baked pastry. Cover and freeze at least 8 hours. Remove from freezer 20–25 minutes before serving.

FROSTY FROZEN STRAWBERRY CRUNCH

1 cup flour
¼ cup brown sugar
½ cup chopped walnuts
½ cup melted butter
2 cups sliced strawberries
2 egg whites
1 cup sugar
2 tbsp. lemon juice
1 cup whipped cream

Combine flour, brown sugar, nuts, and butter. Spread in a shallow pan and bake 20 minutes in a 350-degree oven, stirring occasionally. Combine egg whites, sugar, strawberries, and lemon juice and beat until stiff peaks form, about 10 minutes.

Fold whipped cream into egg white/strawberry mixture. Sprinkle ⅔ of the crumb mixture on the bottom of a 9 × 13-inch pan. Spoon strawberry mixture over crumbs and top with the remaining crumbs. Freeze 6 hours. Garnish with additional strawberries if desired. Store in freezer.

STRAWBERRY SWEETHEARTS

2 pkgs. (3 oz. each) cream cheese
1 cup heavy cream, whipped
1 cup mayonnaise
¼ pound large marshmallaows, finely diced
1 pkg. (12 oz.) frozen strawberries, thawed and drained
1 cup chopped pecans
1 No. 2 can crushed pineapple
⅛ tsp. red food coloring (optional)

Soften cream cheese, using small amount of whipped cream. Fold cream cheese into remaining whipped cream. Fold in remaining ingredients. Pour into refrigerator trays or into 6 or 8 heart-shaped molds. Freeze till firm. Unmold and serve on lettuce, with halved or whole strawberries, if desired.

FROZEN STRAWBERRY DESSERT

2 pkgs. (10 oz.) partially frozen strawberries
1 cup sugar
1 egg white
Juice of 1 lemon
1 pint whipping cream
1 box vanilla wafers, crushed

Beat strawberries, sugar, egg white, and lemon juice at medium speed for 30 minutes. Whip the cream and fold it in the strawberry mixture. Place half the vanilla wafers in a 9 × 13-inch pan; cover with strawberry mixture. Top with remaining vanilla wafers. Freeze for several days. Cut into 15 squares to serve. Yields 15 servings.

STRAWBERRY SQUARES

1 cup sifted all-purpose flour
¼ cup brown sugar
½ cup chopped walnuts
½ cup butter, melted
2 egg whites
1 cup granulated sugar
2 cups sliced strawberries
*   or 1 pkg. (10 oz.) frozen strawberries, thawed*
2 tbsp. lemon juice
1 cup whipping cream

Mix first 4 ingredients. Bake in shallow pan at 350 degrees for 20 minutes, stirring occasionally. Sprinkle ⅔ of the baked crumbs in a 9 × 13-inch pan. Combine egg whites, granulated sugar, berries, and lemon juice. Beat at high speed about 10 minutes. Whip cream and fold in. Spoon mixture over crumbs. Top with remaining crumbs. Freeze 6 hours. Serves 12. Note: If using thawed frozen berries, reduce granulated sugar to ⅔ cup.

STRAWBERRY TARTS

Shells:

Heat oven to 450 degrees. Prepare a favorite pie crust, substituting cream for the water used. Add 2 tablespoons of sugar and ¼ teaspoon of cinnamon. Roll out your pastry so that six 5-inch rounds can be cut. Fit these circles of pie dough over the back of 3-inch muffin cups, pleating the excess dough to fit. Prick the bottoms of shells with a fork. Bake 5 minutes or until golden. Cool on a wire rack.

Cheese coating for bottom of shells:

1 pkg. (8 oz.) cream cheese, softened with
3 tbsp. milk, adding
1 tsp. grated lemon rind and
spoon into cooled shells

160

Filling:

1 quart strawberries, hulled and cored
1 tbsp. lemon juice
½ cup granulated sugar
1 tbsp. cornstarch

In a saucepan, crush one cup of the smaller size strawberries with a wooden spoon and add lemon juice, sugar, and cornstarch. Cook over low heat, stirring, until thickened and clear. Cool. Fold remaining whole berries into the cooked berry mixture until completely covered with glaze.

Carefully remove the strawberries from the sauce and place them over the cream cheese in the shells, dividing strawberries equally among the shells. Distribute remaining syrup over them. Serves 6.

Variation: Use one package vanilla pudding/pie filling as a substitute for the cream cheese.

DELUXE STRAWBERRY TART

1 baked 9-inch pie shell
1 quart strawberries, washed, hulled, and cored
1 pkg. instant vanilla pudding mix
2 cups half-and-half
2 tbsp. Cointreau
1 cup heavy cream, whipped
1 cup currant jelly
4 tbsp. hot water

Prepare pudding mix in a bowl according to directions, substituting half-and-half for milk. Add the Cointreau. Combine the whipped cream with pudding and pour into the pie crust. Arrange unblemished strawberries on top. Melt the jelly with the hot water in a saucepan over low heat and brush over the berries to form a glaze. Serves 6.

STRAWBERRIES AND CREAM TART

1 baked tart (10-inch) or pie crust (9-inch)

Filling:
1 pkg. (8 oz.) cream cheese, softened
⅓ cup sugar
¼ to ½ tsp. almond extract
1 cup heavy cream, whipped
½ cup semisweet chocolate chips
1 tbsp. shortening
4 cups strawberries, washed, hulled, and cored

In a large bowl, beat the cream cheese until fluffy, gradually adding sugar and almond extract. Blend well. Fold in the whipped cream and spoon into the cooled pie crust. Arrange strawberries pointed side up over the filling. Chill.

In a small saucepan, melt chocolate chips and shortening over low heat, stirring constantly until smooth. Drizzle over strawberries and filling. Chill until set. Serves 10–12.

RHUBARB AND STRAWBERRY TART

Your favorite pastry for 1-crust pie
2 cups fresh rhubarb cut into ½-inch cubes
2 cups fresh strawberries, washed, hulled, cored, and cut in half
1 cup sugar
½ tsp. ground cardamom
3 tbsp. flour
2 eggs, slightly beaten
½ cup orange marmalade
1 tbsp. water

Preheat oven to 400 degrees. Place rhubarb and strawberries in a mixing bowl, and add sugar and cardamom blended with flour. Toss. Add eggs and blend thoroughly. Pour mixture into an unbaked pie shell and place on a baking sheet. Bake 40 minutes or until set. Remove and cool. Heat the marmalade with water, stirring until melted. Spoon over pie and smooth it over. Cut into wedges to serve.

STRAWBERRY CHEESE TART

Mellow cream cheese in a sweet crust, topped with fresh red berries and bright green grapes — a large tart that's almost too pretty to eat!

½ recipe cookie crust pastry (recipe below)
1 pkg. (8 oz.) cream cheese, softened
¼ cup heavy cream (or as required)
1½ tbsp. orange juice
1 pint strawberries
½ pound green grapes
¼ cup apple jelly
2 tbsp. sliced almonds, toasted

Cookie crust pastry:
2 cups sifted flour
½ cup sugar
¾ cup (1½ sticks) butter or margarine, softened
2 egg yolks, slightly beaten
1 tsp. vanilla

Mix flour and sugar together in a medium-size bowl. Cut in the butter or margarine with a pastry blender until mixture is crumbly. Add egg yolks and vanilla and mix lightly with a fork just until pastry holds together and leaves side of bowl clean. Chill until ready to use.

Butter the removable bottom of a 9½-inch round, fluted quiche pan. Roll out cookie crust pastry to an 11-inch round on a lightly floured surface. Carefully slip bottom of quiche pan under pastry. Lift the bottom, with pastry, into the pan. Press firmly against sides, turning pastry under to make a stronger edge. Prick bottom and sides well with a fork. Refrigerate 30 minutes. Bake in a hot oven, 400 degrees, for 10 minutes, then lower the heat to 350. Bake 5 minutes longer, or until pastry is golden. Cool thoroughly on a wire rack. Carefully remove side of pan, leaving pastry on removable pan bottom. Place on serving platter. In a small bowl, beat cream cheese with an electric mixer until fluffy. Gradually beat in sugar, cream, and orange juice. Spread over pastry. Refrigerate one hour.

Hull and halve enough strawberries to make one cup. Halve and seed (if necessary) enough grapes to make ¾ cup. Arrange strawberry and grape halves on filling. In a small saucepan, melt jelly over low heat and bring just to boiling. Cool slightly. Brush over fruit to glaze. Refrigerate until ready to serve. Just before serving, sprinkle with almonds.

STRAWBERRY BUTTERCREAM WEDGE TART

1 pkg. (5 oz.) all-ready pie crust (Pillsbury)
2 tsp. flour

Filling:
1 cup butter, softened
2 cups powdered sugar
2 eggs
1 tbsp. cherry-flavored liqueur
2–3 drops red food color, if desired
¼ cup strawberry preserves
2 cups fresh strawberries

Glaze:
Pie crust wedges
Sugar
½ oz. (½ square) semisweet chocolate, chopped
1½ tsp. butter or margarine

Heat oven to 450 degrees. Prepare pie crust according to conventional or microwave package directions for unfilled one-crust pie using a 10-inch tart pan or 9-inch pie pan. Let remaining crust stand at room temperature to make wedges. Place prepared crust in bottom and up sides of pan. Trim edges. Bake at 450 degrees for 9–11 minutes or until lightly browned. Cool.

In a large bowl, beat the butter and powdered sugar until light and fluffy. Add eggs, liqueur, and red food color; beat well. Spread the preserves in the cooled pie crust. Spoon strawberries evenly over the preserves. Spread the filling over the strawberries. Refrigerate while preparing wedges.

To make wedges:
Unfold reserved crust and sprinkle with a heaping teaspoon of flour. Place crust floured side down on an ungreased cookie sheet. Trim crust to a 10-inch circle, then cut into 12 pie-shaped wedges. Sprinkle with sugar. Bake at 450 degrees for 8–11 minutes or until crust is lightly browned. Cool completely. Arrange wedges flat on top of tart, pressing lightly into filling. In a small saucepan over low heat, melt chocolate and butter, stirring constantly until smooth. Drizzle over wedges. Refrigerate for 1–2 hours or until well chilled, then remove sides of pan. Store in refrigerator. Serves 12.

RICE KRISPIE TARTS

2 tbsp. butter or margarine
20 large marshmallows
2½ cups Rice Krispies

Filling:
2 cups whipped cream
1 cup home-frozen strawberries or raspberries, thawed
    or 1 pkg. (15 oz.) commercially frozen strawberries or raspberries,
    thawed and drained

Melt butter or margarine over heat. Add marshmallows. Cook while stirring continually until smooth. Remove from heat. Add Rice Krispies and mix. Butter 12 muffin cups of 2¾-inch size. Use about one heaping tablespoon of mixture per muffin cup. Press into cups to form shells.

For the filling combine the whipped cream and the strawberries or raspberries. Remove shells from muffin pans and fill with the combined whipped cream and fruit. Serves 12.

STRAWBERRY QUICK TARTS
(Carol Shirkey's Tarts)

Spread baked tart shells with commercial pineapple-cream cheese mixture. Fill with strawberries and glaze with melted wild cranberry jelly or currant jelly. Jelly can be heated with a little water to make the glaze.

WILLIAMSBURG QUICK TARTS

1 pkg. (3 oz.) cream cheese
⅓ cup heavy cream

Beat cream cheese with heavy cream. Cream until smooth. Spread the layer in baked tart shells, then add a layer of strawberries or raspberries. Glaze with melted currant jelly.

SECTION INDEX

1. BEVERAGES, DIPS, SPREADS, SAUCES, FONDUES

2. CREPES, CUSTARDS, BARS, MUFFINS, BREAD

3. SOUPS, SANDWICHES, SALADS, PIZZA

4. FRUITS, YOGURTS, DESSERTS

5. PIES, TORTES, JAMS AND JELLIES, CANDIES

6. CAKES, SHORTCAKES, FROSTINGS

6. CAKES, SHORTCAKES, FROSTINGS (Continued)

7. ICE CREAM, SHERBETS, FROZEN DESSERTS, TARTS

7. ICE CREAM, SHERBETS, FROZEN DESSERTS, TARTS (Continued)

GENERAL INDEX